The Lectionary 2008

SPCK

First published in Great Britain in 2007

Society for Promoting Christian Knowledge
36 Causton Street
London SW1P 4ST

Additional material and typographical arrangement
copyright © Society for Promoting Christian Knowledge 2007

All rights reserved. No part of this book may be reproduced or transmitted in any form or by any means, electronic or mechanical, including photocopying, recording, or by any information storage and retrieval system, without permission in writing from the publisher.

British Library Cataloguing-in-Publication Data
A catalogue record for this book is available from the British Library

ISBN 978–0–281–05930–0

1 3 5 7 9 10 8 6 4 2

Typeset by Graphicraft Ltd, Hong Kong
Printed in Great Britain by Ashford Colour Press

CONTENTS

Understanding the Lectionary	4
Making Choices in *Common Worship*	6
Book of Common Prayer	6
Certain Days and Occasions Commonly Observed	7
Key to Liturgical Colours	7
Principal Feasts, Holy Days and Festivals	8
Lesser Festivals and Commemorations	8
Lesser Festivals and Commemorations not observed in 2007–08	9
Common Worship	9
Book of Common Prayer	10
The Common of the Saints	11
Special Occasions	12
The *Common Worship* Calendar and Lectionary (including the Book of Common Prayer Calendar and Lectionary)	14
Calendar 2008	94
Calendar 2009	95

UNDERSTANDING THE

Column 1
The date

Column 3 (Common Worship)
On Principal Feasts, Principal Holy Days, Sundays and Festivals this gives the Principal Service Lectionary, intended for use at the main service of the day (in most churches the mid-morning service), whether or not it is a Eucharist.

On other weekdays this gives the Daily Eucharistic Lectionary for those wanting a semi-continuous pattern of readings and a psalm for Holy Communion. It is most useful in a church where there is a daily celebration and a core community that worships together day by day, though its use is not restricted to that.

Column 4 (Common Worship)
On Principal Feasts, Principal Holy Days, Sundays and Festivals this gives the Third Service Lectionary. Many churches will have no need of it, for it comes into use only if the Principal and Second Service Lectionaries have been used. Its most likely use is at Morning Prayer (when this is not the Principal Service). Where psalms are recommended for use in the morning, these also appear in this column.

On other weekdays this provides the psalmody and readings for Morning Prayer. Where two or more psalms are appointed, the psalm in bold italic may be used as the only psalm. Psalms printed in round brackets ( ) may be omitted if they are used as an opening canticle at Morning Prayer. Where † is printed after the psalm number; the psalm may be shortened if desired. For those wishing to follow the Ordinary Time psalm cycle throughout the year (except for the period between 19 December and the Epiphany and from the Monday of Holy Week to the Saturday of Easter Week), this is printed as an alternative to the seasonal provision.

COMMON WORSHIP January 2008		Sunday Principal Service Weekday Eucharist	Third Service Morning Prayer
12 Sa	**Aelred of Hexham, Abbot of Rievaulx, 1167** Benedict Biscop, Abbot of Wearmouth, Scholar, 689 Com. Religious *also* Ecclus. 15.1–6	or 1 John 5. 14–end Ps. 149. 1–5 John 3. 22–30	Ps. **96**; 145 *alt.* Ps. **76**; 79 Baruch 4. 36 – 5.end or Mic. 5. 2–end Matt. 23. 29–end
13 W S	**THE BAPTISM OF CHRIST**	Isa. 42. 1–9 Ps. 29 Acts 10. 34–43 Matt. 3. 13–end	Ps. 89. 19–29 Exod. 14. 15–22 1 John 5. 6–9
14 DEL 1 M W		1 Sam. 1. 1–8 Ps. 116. 10–15 Mark 1. 14–20	Ps. 2; 110 *alt.* **80**; 82 Gen. 1. 1–19 Matt. 21. 1–17

Week number of Daily Eucharistic Lectionary

Column 2 provides for Common Worship:
- the name of the Principal Holy Day, Sunday, Festival or Lesser Festival;
- a note of other Commemorations for mention in prayers;
- any general note that applies to the whole *Common Worship* provision for the day;
- one of the options where there are two options for readings at the Eucharist or Principal Service;
- an indication of the liturgical colour.

Readings: Readings occur in this column only in two circumstances. On Sundays after Trinity where there are two 'tracks' for the Principal Service readings (where there is a choice of first reading and psalm, but the second reading and Gospel are the same in both tracks), Track 1 appears in this column. On Lesser Festivals throughout the year, where there are readings for that festival that are alternative to the semi-continuous Daily Eucharistic Lectionary, these also appear in this column.

Colour: An upper-case letter indicates the liturgical colour of the day. A lower-case second colour indicates the colour for a Lesser Festival while the upper-case letter indicates the continuing seasonal colour.

LECTIONARY

Column 5 (Common Worship)
On Principal Feasts, Principal Holy Days, Sundays and Festivals this gives the Second Service Lectionary, intended for use when a second set of readings is required. Its most likely use is in the evening, when the Principal Service Lectionary has been used in the morning. Sometimes it might be used at an evening Eucharist. Where the second reading is not a Gospel reading, an alternative to meet this need is provided. Where psalms are recommended for use in the evening, these also appear in this column.

On other weekdays this provides the psalmody and readings for Evening Prayer. Where two or more psalms are provided, the psalm in bold italic may be used as the only psalm. Psalms printed in round brackets ( ) may be omitted if they are used as an opening canticle at Evening Prayer. Where † is printed after the psalm number, the psalm may be shortened if desired. For those wishing to follow the Ordinary Time psalm cycle throughout the year (except for the period between 19 December and the Epiphany and from the Monday of Holy Week to the Saturday of Easter Week), this is printed as an alternative to the seasonal provision.

Column 7 (Book of Common Prayer)
This provides the readings for Morning Prayer, together with psalm provision where it varies from the BCP monthly cycle.

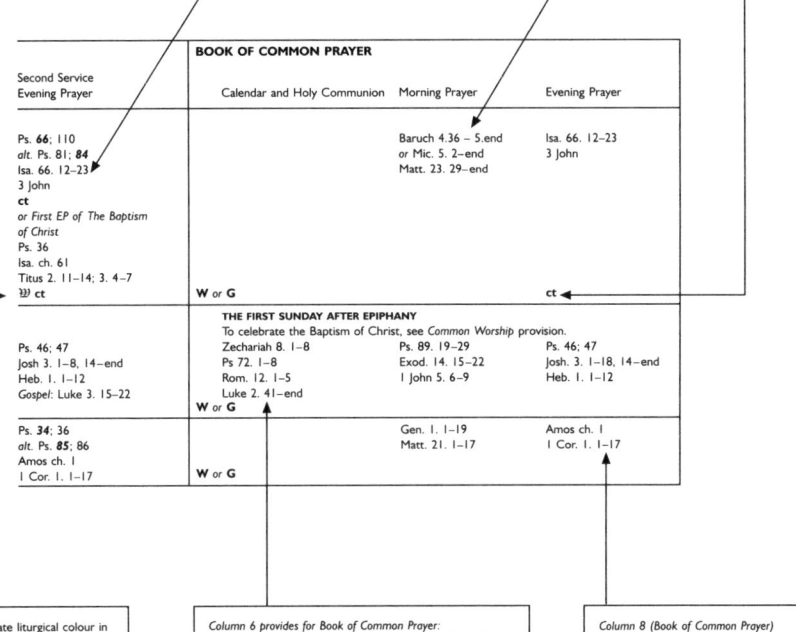

A letter to indicate liturgical colour in this column indicates a change of colour before Evening Prayer. The symbol in bold lower case, **ct**, indicates that the Collect at Evening Prayer should be that of the following day.

Second Service Evening Prayer	BOOK OF COMMON PRAYER		
	Calendar and Holy Communion	Morning Prayer	Evening Prayer
Ps. **66**; 110 alt. Ps. 81; **84** Isa. 66. 12–23 3 John **ct** or First EP of The Baptism of Christ Ps. 36 Isa. ch. 61 Titus 2. 11–14; 3. 4–7 W **ct**		Baruch 4.36 – 5.end or Mic. 5. 2–end Matt. 23. 29–end	Isa. 66. 12–23 3 John **ct**
	THE FIRST SUNDAY AFTER EPIPHANY To celebrate the Baptism of Christ, see *Common Worship* provision.		
Ps. 46; 47 Josh 3. 1–8, 14–end Heb. 1. 1–12 Gospel: Luke 3. 15–22	Zechariah 8. 1–8 Ps 72. 1–8 Rom. 12. 1–5 Luke 2. 41–end **W** or **G**	Ps. 89. 19–29 Exod. 14. 15–22 1 John 5. 6–9	Ps. 46; 47 Josh 3. 1–18, 14–end Heb. 1. 1–12
Ps. **34**; 36 alt. Ps. **85**; 86 Amos ch. 1 1 Cor. 1. 1–17	**W** or **G**	Gen. 1. 1–19 Matt. 21. 1–17	Amos ch. 1 1 Cor. 1. 1–17

A letter to indicate liturgical colour in this column indicates a change of colour before Evening Prayer. The symbol in bold lower case, **ct**, indicates that the Collect at Evening Prayer should be that of the following day.

Column 6 provides for Book of Common Prayer:
- the name of the Principal Holy Day, Sunday, Festival or Lesser Festival;
- any general note that applies to the whole Prayer Book provision for the day and an indication of points at which users may wish to draw on *Common Worship* material on the opposite page where the BCP has no provision;
- the lectionary for the Eucharist on any day for which provision is made;
- an indication of liturgical colour (see column 2).

Column 8 (Book of Common Prayer)
This provides the readings for Evening Prayer, together with psalm provision where it varies from the BCP monthly cycle.

Making Choices in *Common Worship*

Common Worship makes provision for a variety of pastoral and liturgical circumstances. It needs to, for it has to serve some church communities where Morning Prayer, Holy Communion and Evening Prayer are all celebrated every day, and yet be useful also in a church with only one service a week, and that service varying in form and time from week to week.

At the beginning of the year, some decisions in principle need to be taken.

In relation to the Calendar, a decision needs to be taken whether to keep The Presentation of Christ (Candlemas) on Saturday 2 February or on Sunday 3 February, and whether to keep the Feast of All Saints on Saturday 1 November or on Sunday 2 November.

In relation to the Lectionary, the initial choices every year to decide in relation to Sundays are:

- which of the services on a Principal Feast, Principal Holy Day, Sunday or Festival constitutes the 'Principal Service'; then use the Principal Service Lectionary (column 3) consistently for that service through the year;
- during the Sundays after Trinity, whether to use Track 1 of the Principal Service Lectionary (column 2), where the first reading stays over several weeks with one Old Testament book read semi-continuously, or Track 2 (column 3), where the first reading is chosen for its relationship to the Gospel reading of the day;
- which, if any, service on a Principal Feast, Principal Holy Day, Sunday or Festival constitutes the 'Second Service'; then use the Second Service Lectionary (column 5) consistently for that service through the year;
- which, if any, service on a Principal Feast, Principal Holy Day, Sunday or Festival constitutes the 'Third Service'; then use the Third Service Lectionary (column 4) consistently for that service through the year.

And in relation to weekdays:

- whether to use the Daily Eucharistic Lectionary (column 3) consistently for weekday celebrations of Holy Communion (with the exception of Principal Feasts, Principal Holy Days and Festivals) or to make some use of the Lesser Festival provision;
- whether to follow the first psalm provision in column 4 (morning) and column 5 (evening), where psalms during the seasons have a seasonal flavour but in ordinary time follow a sequential pattern; or to follow the alternative provision in the same columns, where psalms follow the sequential pattern throughout the year, except for the period between 19 December and The Epiphany and from the Monday of Holy Week to the Saturday of Easter Week; or to follow the psalm cycle in the Book of Common Prayer, where they are nearly always used 'in course'.

The flexibility of *Common Worship* is intended to enable the church and the minister to find the most helpful provision for them. But once a decision is made, it is advisable to stay with that decision through the year or at the very least through a complete season.

Book of Common Prayer

A separate Lectionary for the Book of Common Prayer is no longer issued. Provision is made on the right-hand pages of this Lectionary for BCP worship on all Sundays in the year, for the major festivals and for Morning and Evening Prayer. The Epistles and Gospels for Holy Communion are those of 1662, with the additions and variations of 1928, now authorized under the *Common Worship* overall provision. The Old Testament readings and psalms for these services, formerly appended to the Series One Holy Communion service, may be used but are not mandatory with the 1662 order.

Readings for Morning and Evening Prayer, which are the same as those for *Common Worship*, are set out in the BCP section for Sundays and weekdays. The special psalm provision of the BCP is given. Otherwise the Psalter is read in course daily through each month.

The Calendar observes BCP dates when these differ from those of *Common Worship*, for example, St Thomas on 21 December. Additional commemorations in the *Common Worship* Calendar are not included, but those who wish to observe them may use the *Collects and Post Communions in Traditional Language: Lesser Festivals, Common of the Saints, Special Occasions* (Church House Publishing).

The Lectionaries of 1871 and 1922, to be found in many copies of the BCP, are still authorized and may be used, but (with the exception of the psalms and readings for Holy Communion mentioned above) the Additional Alternative Lectionary (1961) is no longer authorized for public worship.

Although those who use the BCP, for private or public worship or both, are free to follow any of the authorized lectionaries, there is much to be said for common usage across the Church of England, so that the same passages are being read by all. It is of course appropriate that BCP readings should be taken from the Authorized or King James Version for harmony of style, with the daily recitation of the BCP Psalter.

The integrity of the BCP as the traditional source of worship in the Church of England is not in any way affected by the use of a common lectionary for the daily offices.

CERTAIN DAYS AND OCCASIONS COMMONLY OBSERVED

Plough Sunday may be observed on 13 January 2008.
The Week of Prayer for Christian Unity may be observed from 18 to 25 January 2008.
Education Sunday may be observed on 20 January 2008.
Rogation Sunday may be observed on 27 April 2008.
The Feast of Dedication is observed on the anniversary of the dedication or consecration of a church, or, when the actual date is unknown, on 5 October 2008. In CW 26 October 2008 is an alternative date.
Ember Days. CW encourages the bishop to set the Ember Days in each diocese in the week before the ordinations whereas in BCP the dates are fixed.
Days of Discipline and Self-Denial in CW are the weekdays of Lent and all Fridays in the year, except all Principal Feasts and festivals outside Lent and Fridays between Easter Day and Pentecost. The eves of Principal Feasts are also appropriately kept as days of discipline and self-denial in preparation for the feast.
Days of Fasting and Abstinence according to the BCP are the forty days of Lent, the Ember Days at the four seasons, the three Rogation Days, and all Fridays in the year except Christmas Day. The BCP also orders the observance of the Evens or Vigils before The Nativity of our Lord, The Purification of the Blessed Virgin Mary, The Annunciation of the Blessed Virgin Mary, Easter Day, Ascension Day, Pentecost, and before the following saints' days: Matthias, John the Baptist, Peter, James, Bartholomew, Matthew, Simon and Jude, Andrew, Thomas, and All Saints. (If any of these days falls on Monday, the Vigil is to be kept on the previous Saturday.)

KEY TO LITURGICAL COLOURS

Common Worship suggests appropriate liturgical colours. They are not mandatory and traditional or local use may be followed.

For a detailed discussion of when colours may be used see *Common Worship: Services and Prayers for the Church of England* (Church House Publishing), *New Handbook of Pastoral Liturgy* (SPCK) or *A Companion to Common Worship: Volume I* (SPCK).

W	White
W	Gold or white
R	Red
P	Purple (may vary from 'Roman purple' to violet, with blue as an alternative; a Lent array of sackcloth may be used in Lent, and rose pink on The Third Sunday of Advent and Fourth Sunday of Lent)
G	Green

When a lower-case letter accompanies an upper-case letter, the lower-case letter indicates the liturgical colour appropriate to the Lesser Festival of that day, while the upper-case letter indicates the continuing seasonal colour.

PRINCIPAL FEASTS, HOLY DAYS AND FESTIVALS

Principal Feasts, and other principal Holy Days (Ash Wednesday, Maundy Thursday, Good Friday), are printed in **LARGE BOLD CAPITALS** in the Lectionary.

All Saints' Day is celebrated on either 1 November or the Sunday between 30 October and 5 November.

There are no longer proper readings relating to the Holy Spirit on the six days after Pentecost. Instead they have been located on the nine days before Pentecost.

When Patronal and Dedication Festivals are kept as Principal Feasts, they may be transferred to the nearest Sunday, unless that day is already either a Principal Feast or The First Sunday of Advent, The Baptism of Christ, The First Sunday of Lent or Palm Sunday.

Festivals are printed in the Lectionary in SMALL BOLD CAPITALS.

For each day there is a full liturgical provision for the Holy Communion and for Morning and Evening Prayer. Most holy days that are in the category 'Festival' are provided with an optional First Evening Prayer. Its use is entirely at the discretion of the minister. Where it is used, the liturgical colour for the next day should be used at that First Evening Prayer and this has been indicated in the provision on the following pages.

LESSER FESTIVALS AND COMMEMORATIONS

Lesser Festivals (printed in **bold roman** typeface) are observed at the level appropriate to a particular church. The readings and psalms for The Common of the Saints are listed on page 11. In addition, there are special readings appropriate to the Festival listed in the first column. The daily psalms and readings at Morning and Evening Prayer are not usually superseded by those for Lesser Festivals, but the readings and psalms for Holy Communion may on occasion be used at Morning or Evening Prayer.

Commemorations are printed in the Lectionary in *italic* typeface. They do not have collect, psalm or readings, but may be observed by mention in prayers of intercession and thanksgiving. For local reasons, or where there is an established tradition in the wider Church, they may be kept as Lesser Festivals using the appropriate material from The Common of the Saints. Equally, it may be desirable to observe some Lesser Festivals as Commemorations.

If a Lesser Festival or a Commemoration falls on a Principal Feast, Principal Holy Day, Sunday or Festival, it is not normally observed that year, although it may be celebrated, where there is sufficient reason, on the nearest available day. Lesser Festivals and Commemorations which, for this reason, would not be celebrated in 2007–08 are listed on pages 9–10, so that, if desired, they may be memtioned in prayers of intercession and thanksgiving.

LESSER FESTIVALS AND COMMEMORATIONS NOT OBSERVED IN 2007-08

The Lesser Festivals and Commemorations (shown in italics) listed below fall on a Sunday or during Holy Week or Easter Week this year, and are thus not observed in this lectionary.

Common Worship

2008

January
13   Hilary, Bishop of Poitiers, Teacher, 367
      Kentigern (Mungo), Missionary Bishop in Strathclyde and Cumbria, 603
      George Fox, Founder of the Society of Friends (the Quakers), 1691
20   *Richard Rolle of Hampole, Spiritual Writer, 1349*

February
3   Anskar, Archbishop of Hamburg, Missionary in Denmark and Sweden, 865
6   *The Martyrs of Japan, 1597*
10   *Scholastica, sister of Benedict, Abbess of Plombariola, c. 543*
17   Janani Luwum, Archbishop of Uganda, 1977

March
2   Chad, Bishop of Lichfield, Missionary, 672
17   Patrick, Bishop, Missionary, Patron of Ireland, c. 460
18   *Cyril, Bishop of Jerusalem, Teacher, 386*
20   Cuthbert, Bishop of Lindisfarne, Missionary, 687
21   Thomas Cranmer, Archbishop of Canterbury, Reformation Martyr, 1556
24   *Walter Hilton of Thurgarton, Augustinian Canon, Mystic, 1396*
      Oscar Romero, Archbishop of San Salvador, Martyr, 1980
26   *Harriet Monsell, Founder of the Community of St John the Baptist, Clewer, 1883*
31   *John Donne, Priest, Poet, 1631*

April
1   *Frederick Denison Maurice, Priest, Teacher, 1872*
27   *Christina Rossetti, Poet, 1894*

May
2   Athanasius, Bishop of Alexandria, Teacher, 373
4   English Saints and Martyrs of the Reformation Era
25   The Venerable Bede, Monk at Jarrow, Scholar, Historian, 735
      Aldhelm, Bishop of Sherborne, 709

June
1   Justin, Martyr at Rome, c. 165
8   Thomas Ken, Bishop of Bath and Wells, Non-Juror, Hymn Writer, 1711
15   *Evelyn Underhill, Spiritual Writer, 1941*
22   Alban, first Martyr of Britain, c. 250

July
6   *Thomas More, Scholar, and John Fisher, Bishop of Rochester, Reformation Martyrs, 1535*
20   *Margaret of Antioch, Martyr, 4th century*
      Bartolomé de las Casas, Apostle to the Indies, 1566
27   *Brooke Foss Westcott, Bishop of Durham, Teacher, 1901*

August
10	Laurence, Deacon at Rome, Martyr, 258
31	Aidan, Bishop of Lindisfarne, Missionary, 651

October
12	Wilfrid of Ripon, Bishop, Missionary, 709
	Elizabeth Fry, Prison Reformer, 1845
	Edith Cavell, Nurse, 1915
19	Henry Martyn, Translator of the Scriptures, Missionary in India and Persia, 1812
26	Alfred the Great, King of the West Saxons, Scholar, 899
	Cedd, Abbot of Lastingham, Bishop of the East Saxons, 664

November
2	Commemoration of the Faithful Departed (All Souls' Day)
9	*Margery Kempe, Mystic, c. 1440*
16	Margaret, Queen of Scotland, Philanthropist, Reformer of the Church, 1093
	Edmund Rich of Abingdon, Archbishop of Canterbury, 1240
23	Clement, Bishop of Rome, Martyr, c. 100

December
1	*Charles de Foucauld, Hermit in the Sahara, 1916*
7	Ambrose, Bishop of Milan, Teacher, 397
14	John of the Cross, Poet, Teacher, 1591

Book of Common Prayer

2008

January
13	Hilary, Bishop of Poitiers, Teacher, 367
20	Fabian, Bishop of Rome, Martyr, 250

February
3	Blasius, Bishop of Sebastopol, Martyr, c. 316

March
2	Chad, Bishop of Lichfield, Missionary, 672
18	Edward, King of the W. Saxons, 978
21	Benedict, Abbot of Monte Cassino, c. 550

June
1	Nicomede, Priest and Martyr at Rome (date unknown)

July
20	Margaret of Antioch, Martyr, 4th century

August
10	Laurence, Deacon at Rome, Martyr, 258

September
7	Evurtius, Bishop of Orleans, 4th century
14	Holy Cross Day

November
23	Clement, Bishop of Rome, Martyr, c. 100

THE COMMON OF THE SAINTS

The Blessed Virgin Mary
Genesis 3. 8–15, 20; Isaiah 7. 10–14; Micah 5. 1–4
Acts 1. 12–14; Romans 8. 18–30; Galatians 4. 4–7
Psalms 45. 10–17; 113; 131
Luke 1. 26–38; Luke 1. 39–47; John 19. 25–27

Martyrs
2 Chronicles 24. 17–21; Isaiah 43. 1–7; Jeremiah 11. 18–20; Wisdom 4. 10–15
Romans 8. 35–end; 2 Corinthians 4. 7–15; 2 Timothy 2. 3–7 [8–13]; Hebrews 11. 32–end; 1 Peter 4. 12–end; Revelation 12. 10–12a
Psalms 3; 11; 31. 1–5; 44. 18–24; 126
Matthew 10. 16–22; Matthew 10. 28–39; Matthew 16. 24–26; John 12. 24–26; John 15. 18–21

Teachers of the Faith and Spiritual Writers
1 Kings 3. [6–10] 11–14; Proverbs 4. 1–9; Wisdom 7. 7–10, 15–16; Ecclesiasticus 39. 1–10
1 Corinthians 1. 18–25; 1 Corinthians 2. 1–10; 1 Corinthians 2. 9–end;
Ephesians 3. 8–12; 2 Timothy 4. 1–8; Titus 2. 1–8
Psalms 19. 7–10; 34. 11–17; 37. 31–35; 119. 89–96; 119. 97–104
Matthew 5. 13–19; Matthew 13. 52–end; Matthew 23. 8–12; Mark 4. 1–9; John 16. 12–15

Bishops and Other Pastors
1 Samuel 16. 1, 6–13; Isaiah 6. 1–8; Jeremiah 1. 4–10; Ezekiel 3. 16–21; Malachi 2. 5–7
Acts 20. 28–35; 1 Corinthians 4. 1–5; 2 Corinthians 4. 1–10 (or 1–2, 5–7); 2 Corinthians 5. 14–20; 1 Peter 5. 1–4
Psalms 1; 15; 16. 5–end; 96; 110
Matthew 11. 25–end; Matthew 24. 42–46; John 10. 11–16; John 15. 9–17; John 21. 15–17

Members of Religious Communities
1 Kings 19. 9–18; Proverbs 10. 27–end; Song of Solomon 8. 6–7; Isaiah 61.10 – 62.5; Hosea 2. 14–15, 19–20
Acts 4. 32–35; 2 Corinthians 10.17 – 11.2; Philippians 3. 7–14; 1 John 2. 15–17; Revelation 19. 1, 5–9
Psalms 34. 1–8; 112. 1–9; 119. 57–64; 123; 131
Matthew 11. 25–end; Matthew 19. 3–12; Matthew 19. 23–end; Luke 9. 57–end; Luke 12. 32–37

Missionaries
Isaiah 52. 7–10; Isaiah 61. 1–3a; Ezekiel 34. 11–16; Jonah 3. 1–5
Acts 2. 14, 22–36; Acts 13. 46–49; Acts 16. 6–10; Acts 26. 19–23; Romans 15. 17–21; 2 Corinthians 5.11 – 6.2
Psalms 67; 87; 97; 100; 117
Matthew 9. 35–end; Matthew 28. 16–end; Mark 16. 15–20; Luke 5. 1–11; Luke 10. 1–9

Any Saint
Genesis 12. 1–4; Proverbs 8. 1–11; Micah 6. 6–8; Ecclesiasticus 2. 7–13 [14–end]
Ephesians 3. 14–19; Ephesians 6. 11–18; Hebrews 13. 7–8, 15–16; James 2. 14–17; 1 John 4. 7–16; Revelation 21. [1–4] 5–7
Psalms 32; 33. 1–5; 119. 1–8; 139. 1–4 [5–12]; 145. 8–14
Matthew 19. 16–21; Matthew 25. 1–13; Matthew 25. 14–30; John 15. 1–8; John 17. 20–end

SPECIAL OCCASIONS

The Guidance of the Holy Spirit
Proverbs 24. 3–7; Isaiah 30. 15–21; Wisdom 9. 13–17
Acts 15. 23–29; Romans 8. 22–27; 1 Corinthians 12. 4–13
Psalms 25. 1–9; 104. 26–33; 143. 8–10
Luke 14. 27–33; John 14. 23–26; John 16. 13–15

The Commemoration of the Faithful Departed
Lamentations 3. 17–26, 31–33 or Wisdom 3. 1–9
Psalm 23 or Psalm 27. 1–6, 16–end
Romans 5. 5–11 or 1 Peter 1. 3–9
John 5. 19–25 or John 6. 37–40

Rogation Days
Deuteronomy 8. 1–10; 1 Kings 8. 35–40; Job 28. 1–11
Philippians 4. 4–7; 2 Thessalonians 3. 6–13; 1 John 5. 12–15
Psalms 104. 21–30; 107. 1–9; 121
Matthew 6. 1–15; Mark 11. 22–24; Luke 11. 5–13

Harvest Thanksgiving
Year A
Deuteronomy 8. 7–18 or Deuteronomy 28. 1–14
Psalm 65
2 Corinthians 9. 6–end
Luke 12. 16–30 or Luke 17. 11–19

Year B
Joel 2. 21–27
Psalm 126
1 Timothy 2. 1–7 or 1 Timothy 6. 6–10
Matthew 6. 25–33

Year C
Deuteronomy 26. 1–11
Psalm 100
Philippians 4. 4–9 or Revelation 14. 14–18
John 6. 25–35

Mission and Evangelism
Isaiah 49. 1–6; Isaiah 52. 7–10; Micah 4. 1–5
Acts 17. 12–end; 2 Corinthians 5.14 – 6.2; Ephesians 2. 13–end
Psalms 2; 46; 67
Matthew 5. 13–16; Matthew 28. 16–end; John 17. 20–end

The Unity of the Church
Jeremiah 33. 6–9a; Ezekiel 36. 23–28; Zephaniah 3. 16–end
Ephesians 4. 1–6; Colossians 3. 9–17; 1 John 4. 9–15
Psalms 100; 122; 133
Matthew 18. 19–22; John 11. 45–52; John 17. 11b–23

The Peace of the World
Isaiah 9. 1–6; Isaiah 57. 15–19; Micah 4. 1–5
Philippians 4. 6–9; 1 Timothy 2. 1–6; James 3. 13–18
Psalms 40. 14–17; 72. 1–7; 85. 8–13
Matthew 5. 43–end; John 14. 23–29; John 15. 9–17

Social Justice and Responsibility
Isaiah 32. 15–end; Amos 5. 21–24; Amos 8. 4–7; Acts 5. 1–11
Colossians 3. 12–15; James 2. 1–4
Psalms 31. 21–24; 85. 1–7; 146. 5–10
Matthew 5. 1–12; Matthew 25. 31–end; Luke 16. 19–end

Ministry (including Ember Days)
Numbers 11. 16–17, 24–29; Numbers 27. 15–end; 1 Samuel 16. 1–13a
Isaiah 6. 1–8; Isaiah 61. 1–3; Jeremiah 1. 4–10
Acts 20. 28–35; 1 Corinthians 3. 3–11; Ephesians 4. 4–16; Philippians 3. 7–14
Psalms 40. 8–13; 84. 8–12; 89. 19–25; 101. 1–5, 7; 122
Luke 4. 16–21; Luke 12. 35–43; Luke 22. 24–27; John 4. 31–38; John 15. 5–17

In Time of Trouble
Genesis 9. 8–17; Job 1. 13–end; Isaiah 38. 6–11
Romans 3. 21–26; Romans 8. 18–25; 2 Corinthians 8. 1–5, 9
Psalms 86. 1–7; 107. 4–15; 142. 1–7
Mark 4. 35–end; Luke 12. 1–7; John 16. 31–end

For the Sovereign
Joshua 1. 1–9; Proverbs 8. 1–16
Romans 13. 1–10; Revelation 21.22 – 22.4
Psalms 20; 101; 121
Matthew 22. 16–22; Luke 22. 24–30

December 2007

			Sunday Principal Service / Weekday Eucharist	Third Service / Morning Prayer
2	S	**THE FIRST SUNDAY OF ADVENT** CW Year A begins	Isa. 2. 1–5 Ps. 122 Rom. 13. 11–end	Ps. 44 Micah 4. 1–7 1 Thess. 5. 1–11
	P		Matt. 24. 36–44	
3	M	Francis Xavier, Missionary, Apostle of the Indies, 1552 Daily Eucharistic Lectionary Year 2 begins	Isa. 4. 2–end Ps. 122 Matt. 8. 5–11	Ps. *50*; 54 alt. Ps. *1*; 2; 3 Isa. 25. 1–9
	P			Matt. 12. 1–21
4	Tu	John of Damascus, Monk, Teacher, c. 749; Nicholas Ferrar, Deacon, Founder of the Little Gidding Community, 1637		
			Isa. 11. 1–10 Ps. 72. 1–4, 18–19 Luke 10. 21–24	Ps. *80*; 82 alt. Ps. *5*; 6; (8) Isa. 26. 1–13
	P			Matt. 12. 22–37
5	W		Isa. 25. 6–10a Ps. 23 Matt. 15. 29–37	Ps. 5; *7* alt. Ps. 119. 1–32 Isa. 28. 1–13
	P			Matt. 12. 38–end
6	Th	**Nicholas, Bishop of Myra, c. 326** Com. Bishop or also Isa. 61. 1–3 1 Tim. 6. 6–11	Isa. 26. 1–6 Ps. 118. 18–27a Matt. 7. 21, 24–27	Ps. *42*; 43 alt. Ps. 14; *15*; 16 Isa. 28. 14–end
	Pw	Mark 10. 13–16		Matt. 13. 1–23
7	F	**Ambrose, Bishop of Milan, Teacher, 397** Com. Teacher or also Isa. 41. 9b–13 Luke 22. 24–30	Isa. 29. 17–end Ps. 27. 1–4, 16–17 Matt. 9. 27–31	Ps. *25*; 26 alt. Ps. 17; *19* Isa. 29. 1–14
	Pw			Matt. 13. 24–43
8	Sa	**The Conception of the Blessed Virgin Mary** Com. BVM or	Isa. 30. 19–21, 23–26 Ps. 146. 4–9 Matt. 9.35 – 10.1, 6–8	Ps. *9* (10) alt. Ps. 20; 21; *23* Isa. 29. 15–end
	Pw			Matt. 13. 44–end
9	S	**THE SECOND SUNDAY OF ADVENT**	Isa. 11. 1–10 Ps. 72. 1–7 [18–19] Rom. 15. 4–13	Ps. 80 Amos ch. 7 Luke 1. 5–20
	P		Matt. 3. 1–12	
10	M		Isa. ch. 35 Ps. 85. 7–end Luke 5. 17–26	Ps. 44 alt. Ps. 27; *30* Isa. 30. 1–18
	P			Matt. 14. 1–12
11	Tu		Isa. 40. 1–11 Ps. 96. 1, 10–end Matt. 18. 12–14	Ps. *56*; 57 alt. Ps. 32; *36* Isa. 30. 19–end
	P			Matt. 14. 13–end
12	W	Ember Day*	Isa. 40. 25–end Ps. 103. 8–13 Matt. 11. 28–end	Ps. *62*; 63 alt. Ps. 34 Isa. ch. 31
	P			Matt. 15. 1–20
13	Th	**Lucy, Martyr at Syracuse, 304** Samuel Johnson, Moralist, 1784 Com. Martyr or also Wisd. 3. 1–7	Isa. 41. 13–20 Ps. 145. 1, 8–13	Ps. 53; *54*; 60 alt. Ps. 37† Isa. ch. 32
	Pr	2 Cor. 4. 6–15	Matt. 11. 11–15	Matt. 15. 21–28

*For Ember Day provision, see p. 13.

BOOK OF COMMON PRAYER

Second Service Evening Prayer	Calendar and Holy Communion	Morning Prayer	Evening Prayer
	THE FIRST SUNDAY IN ADVENT Advent I Collect until Christmas Eve		
Ps. 9. 1–8 [9–end] Isa. 52. 1–12 Matt. 24. 15–28	Mic. 4. 1–4, 6–7 Ps. 25. 1–9 Rom. 13. 8–14 Matt. 21. 1–13 P	Ps. 44 Isa. 2. 1–5 1 Thess. 5. 1–11	Ps. 9. 1–8 [9–end] Isa. 52. 1–12 Matt. 24. 15–28
Ps. 70; *71* alt. Ps. *4*; 7 Isa. 42. 18–end Rev. ch. 19	P	Isa. 25. 1–9 Matt. 12. 1–21	Isa. 42. 18–end Rev. ch. 19
Ps. *74*; 75 alt. *9*; 10† Isa. 43. 1–13 Rev. ch. 20	P	Isa. 26. 1–13 Matt. 12. 22–37	Isa. 43. 1–13 Rev. ch. 20
Ps. 76; *77* alt. Ps. *11*; 12; 13 Isa. 43. 14–end Rev. 21. 1–8	P	Isa. 28. 1–13 Matt. 12. 38–end	Isa. 43. 14–end Rev. 21. 1–8
Ps. *40*; 46 alt. Ps. 18† Isa. 44. 1–8 Rev. 21. 9–21	**Nicholas, Bishop of Myra, c. 326** Com. Bishop Pw	Isa. 28. 14–end Matt. 13. 1–23	Isa. 44. 1–8 Rev. 21. 9–21
Ps. 16; *17* alt. Ps. 22 Isa. 44. 9–23 Rev. 21.22 – 22.5	P	Isa. 29. 1–14 Matt. 13. 24–43	Isa. 44. 9–23 Rev. 21.22 – 22.5
Ps. *27*; 28 alt. Ps. *24*; 25 Isa. 44.24 – 45.13 Rev. 22. 6–end ct	**The Conception of the Blessed Virgin Mary** Pw	Isa. 29. 15–end Matt. 13. 44–end	Isa. 44.24 – 45.13 Rev. 22. 6–end ct
	THE SECOND SUNDAY IN ADVENT 2 Kings 22. 8–10; 23. 1–3		
Ps. 11 [28] 1 Kings 18. 17–39 John 1. 19–28	Ps. 50. 1–6 Rom. 15. 4–13 Luke 21. 25–33 P	Ps. 80 Amos ch. 7 Luke 1. 5–20	Ps. 11 [28] 1 Kings 18. 17–39 Matt. 3. 1–12
Ps. *144*; 146 alt. Ps. 26; *28*; 29 Isa. 45. 14–end 1 Thess. ch. 1	P	Isa. 30. 1–18 Matt. 14. 1–12	Isa. 45. 14–end 1 Thess. ch. 1
Ps. *11*; 12; 13 alt. Ps. 33 Isa. ch. 46 1 Thess. 2. 1–12	P	Isa. 30. 19–end Matt. 14. 13–end	Isa. ch. 46 1 Thess. 2. 1–12
Ps. *10*; 14 alt. Ps. 119. 33–56 Isa. ch. 47 1 Thess. 2. 13–end	P	Isa. ch. 31 Matt. 15. 1–20	Isa. ch. 47 1 Thess. 2. 13–end
Ps. 73 alt. Ps. 39; *40* Isa. 48. 1–11 1 Thess. ch. 3	**Lucy, Martyr at Syracuse, 304** Com. Virgin Martyr Pr	Isa. ch. 32 Matt. 15. 21–28	Isa. 48. 1–11 1 Thess. ch. 3

December 2007

			Sunday Principal Service / Weekday Eucharist	Third Service / Morning Prayer
14	F Pw	**John of the Cross, Poet, Teacher, 1591** Ember Day* Com. Teacher *or* *esp.* 1 Cor. 2. 1–10 *also* John 14. 18–23	Isa. 48. 17–19 Ps. 1 Matt. 11. 16–19	Ps. 85; **86** *alt.* Ps. 31 Isa. 33. 1–22 Matt. 15. 29–end
15	Sa P	Ember Day*	Ecclus. 48. 1–4, 9–11 *or* 2 Kings 2. 9–12 Ps. 80. 1–4, 18–19 Matt. 17. 10–13	Ps. 145 *alt.* Ps. 41; **42**; 43 Isa. ch. 35 Matt. 16. 1–12
16	S P	**THE THIRD SUNDAY OF ADVENT**	Isa. ch. 35 Ps. 146. 4–10 *or Canticle:* Magnificat James 5. 7–10 Matt. 11. 2–11	Ps. 68. 1–19 Zeph. 3. 14–end Phil. 4. 4–7
17	M P	O Sapientia *Eglantyne Jebb, Social Reformer, Founder of 'Save the Children', 1928*	Gen. 49. 2, 8–10 Ps. 72. 1–5, 18–19 Matt. 1. 1–17	Ps. 40 *alt.* Ps. 44 Isa. 38. 1–8, 21–22 Matt. 16. 13–end
18	Tu P		Jer. 23. 5–8 Ps. 72. 1–2, 12–13, 18–end Matt. 1. 18–24	Ps. **70**; 74 *alt.* Ps. **48**; 52 Isa. 38. 9–20 Matt. 17. 1–13
19	W P		Judg. 13. 2–7, 24–end Ps. 71. 3–8 Luke 1. 5–25	Ps. 144; **146** Isa. ch. 39 Matt. 17. 14–21
20	Th P		Isa. 7. 10–14 Ps. 24. 1–6 Luke 1. 26–38	Ps. **46**; 95 Zeph. 1.1 – 2.3 Matt. 17. 22–end
21	F** P		Zeph. 3. 14–18 Ps. 33. 1–4, 11–12, 20–end Luke 1. 39–45	Ps. **121**; 122; 123 Zeph. 3. 1–13 Matt. 18. 1–20
22	Sa P		1 Sam. 1. 24–end Ps. 113 Luke 1. 46–56	Ps. **124**; 125; 126; 127 Zeph. 3. 14–end Matt. 18. 21–end
23	S P	**THE FOURTH SUNDAY OF ADVENT**	Isa. 7. 10–16 Ps. 80. 1–8 [18–20] Rom. 1. 1–7 Matt. 1. 18–end	Ps. 144 Micah 5. 2–5a Luke 1. 26–38
24	M P	**CHRISTMAS EVE**	*Morning Eucharist* 2 Sam. 7. 1–5, 8–11, 16 Ps. 89. 2, 19–27 Acts 13. 16–26 Luke 1. 67–79	Ps. **45**; 113 Mal. 1. 1, 6–end Matt. 19. 1–12

*For Ember Day provision, see page 13.
**Thomas the Apostle may be celebrated on 21 December instead of 3 July.

BOOK OF COMMON PRAYER

Second Service Evening Prayer	Calendar and Holy Communion	Morning Prayer	Evening Prayer
Ps. 82; **90** alt. Ps. 35 Isa. 48. 12–end 1 Thess. 4. 1–12	P	Isa. 33. 1–22 Matt. 15. 29–end	Isa. 48. 12–end 1 Thess. 4. 1–12
Ps. 93; **94** alt. Ps. 45; **46** Isa. 49. 1–13 1 Thess. 4. 13–end ct	P	Isa. ch. 35 Matt. 16. 1–12	Isa. 49. 1–13 1 Thess. 4. 13–end ct
Ps. 12 [14] Isa. 5. 8–end Acts 13. 13–41 Gospel: John 5. 31–40	**THE THIRD SUNDAY IN ADVENT** O Sapientia Isa. ch. 35 Ps. 80. 1–7 1 Cor. 4. 1–5 Matt. 11. 2–10 P	Ps. 68. 1–19 Zeph. 3. 14–end James 5. 7–10	Ps. 12 [14] Isa. 5. 8–end Acts 13. 13–41
Ps. 25; **26** alt. Ps. **47**; 49 Isa. 49. 14–25 1 Thess. 5. 1–11	P	Isa. 38. 1–8, 21–22 Matt. 16. 13–end	Isa. 49. 14–25 1 Thess. 5. 1–11
Ps. **50**; 54 alt. Ps. 50 Isa. ch. 50 1 Thess. 5. 12–end	P	Isa. 38. 9–20 Matt. 17. 1–13	Isa. ch. 50 1 Thess. 5. 12–end
Ps. 10; **57** Isa. 51. 1–8 2 Thess. ch. 1	Ember Day Ember CEG P	Isa. ch. 39 Matt. 17. 14–21	Isa. 51. 1–8 2 Thess. ch. 1
Ps. **4**; 9 Isa. 51. 9–16 2 Thess. ch. 2	P	Zeph. 1.1 – 2.3 Matt. 17. 22–end	Isa. 51. 9–16 2 Thess. ch. 2 or First EP of Thomas (Ps. 27) Isa. ch. 35 Heb. 10.35 – 11.1 R ct
Ps. 80; **84** Isa. 51. 17–end 2 Thess. ch. 3	**THOMAS THE APOSTLE** Ember Day Job 42. 1–6 Ps. 139. 1–11 Eph. 2. 19–end John 20. 24–end R	(Ps. 92; 146) 2 Sam. 15. 17–21 or Ecclus. ch. 2 John 11. 1–16	(Ps. 139) Hab. 2. 1–4 1 Pet. 1. 3–12
Ps. 24; **48** Isa. 52. 1–12 Jude ct	Ember Day Ember CEG P	Zeph. 3. 14–end Matt. 18. 21–end	Isa. 52. 1–12 Jude ct
Ps. 113 [126] 1 Sam 1. 1–20 Rev. 22. 6–end Gospel: Luke 1. 39–45	**THE FOURTH SUNDAY IN ADVENT** Isa. 40. 1–9 Ps. 145. 17–end Phil. 4. 4–7 John 1. 19–28 P	Ps. 144 Micah 5. 2–5a Luke 1. 26–38	Ps. 113 [126] 1 Sam 1. 1–20 Rev. 22. 6–end
Ps. 85 Zech. ch. 2 Rev. 1. 1–8	**CHRISTMAS EVE** Coll. (1) Christmas Eve (2) Advent 1 Mic. 5. 2–5a Ps. 24 Titus 3. 3–7 Luke 2. 1–14 P	Ps. **45**; 113 Mal. 1. 1, 6–end Matt. 19. 1–12	Ps. 85 Zech. ch. 2 Rev. 1. 1–8

December 2007

			Sunday Principal Service / Weekday Eucharist	Third Service / Morning Prayer
25	Tu	**CHRISTMAS DAY** Any of the following sets of readings may be used on the evening of Christmas Eve and on Christmas Day. Set III should be used at some service during the celebration.	*I* Isa. 9. 2–7 Ps. 96 Titus 2. 11–14 Luke 2. 1–14 [15–20] *II* Isa. 62. 6–end Ps. 97 Titus 3. 4–7 Luke 2. [1–7] 8–20 *III* Isa. 52. 7–10 Ps. 98 Heb. 1. 1–4 [5–12] John 1. 1–14	MP: Ps. *110*; 117 Isa. 62. 1–5 Matt. 1. 18–end
	W			
26	W	**STEPHEN, DEACON, FIRST MARTYR** The reading from Acts must be used as either the first or second reading at the Eucharist.	2 Chron. 24. 20–22 or Acts 7. 51–end Ps. 119. 161–168 Acts 7. 51–end or Gal. 2. 16b–20 Matt. 10. 17–22	MP: Ps. *13*; 31. 1–8; 150 Jer. 26. 12–15 Acts ch. 6
	R			
27	Th	**JOHN, APOSTLE AND EVANGELIST**	Exod. 33. 7–11a Ps. 117 1 John ch. 1 John 21. 19b–end	MP: Ps. *21*; 147. 13–end Exod. 33. 12–end 1 John 2. 1–11
	W			
28	F	**THE HOLY INNOCENTS**	Jer. 31. 15–17 Ps. 124 1 Cor. 1. 26–29 Matt. 2. 13–18	MP: Ps. *36*; 146 Baruch 4. 21–27 or Gen. 37. 13–20 Matt. 18. 1–10
	R			
29	Sa	**Thomas Becket, Archbishop of Canterbury, Martyr, 1170*** Com. Martyr or *esp.* Matt. 10. 28–33 *also* Ecclus. 51. 1–8	1 John 2. 3–11 Ps. 96. 1–4 Luke 2. 22–35	Ps. *19*; 20 Jonah ch. 1 Col. 1. 1–14
	Wr			
30	S	**THE FIRST SUNDAY OF CHRISTMAS**	Isa. 63. 7–9 Ps. 148. [1–6] 7–end Heb. 2. 10–end Matt. 2. 13–end	Ps. 105. 1–11 Isa. 35. 1–6 Gal. 3. 23–end
	W			
31	M	John Wyclif, Reformer, 1384	1 John 2. 18–21 Ps. 96. 1, 11–end John 1. 1–18	Ps. 102 Jonah chs 3 and 4 Col. 1.24 – 2.7
	W			

*Thomas Becket may be celebrated on 7 July instead of 29 December.

BOOK OF COMMON PRAYER

Second Service Evening Prayer		Calendar and Holy Communion	Morning Prayer	Evening Prayer
EP: Ps. 8 Isa. 65. 17–25 Phil. 2. 5–11 or Luke 2. 1–20 *if it has not been used at the principal service of the day*	₩	**CHRISTMAS DAY** Isa. 9. 2–7 Ps. 98 Heb. 1. 1–12 John 1. 1–14	Ps. 110; 117 Isa. 62. 1–5 Matt. 1. 18–end	Ps. 8 Isa. 65. 17–25 Phil. 2. 5–11 or Luke 2. 1–20
EP: Ps. 57; **86** Gen. 4. 1–10 Matt. 23. 34–end	R	**STEPHEN, DEACON, FIRST MARTYR** Collect (1) Stephen (2) Christmas 2 Chron. 24. 20–22 Ps. 119. 161–168 Acts 7. 55–end Matt. 23. 34–end	(Ps. 13; 31. 1–8; 150) Jer. 26. 12–15 Acts ch. 6	(Ps. 57; 86) Gen. 4. 1–10 Matt. 10. 17–22
EP: Ps. 97 Isa. 6. 1–8 1 John 5. 1–12	W	**JOHN, APOSTLE AND EVANGELIST** Collect (1) John (2) Christmas Exod. 33. 18–end Ps. 92. 11–end 1 John ch. 1 John 21. 19b–end	(Ps. 21; 147. 13–end) Exod. 33. 7–11a 1 John 2. 1–11	(Ps. 97) Isa. 6. 1–8 1 John 5. 1–12
EP: Ps. 123; **128** Isa. 49. 14–25 Mark 10. 13–16	R	**THE HOLY INNOCENTS** Collect (1) Innocents (2) Christmas Jer. 31. 10–17 Ps. 123 Rev. 14. 1–5 Matt. 2. 13–18	(Ps. 36; 146) Baruch 4. 21–27 or Gen. 37. 13–20 Matt. 18. 1–10	(Ps. 124; 128) Isa. 49. 14–25 Mark 10. 13–16
Ps. 131; **132** Isa. 57. 15–end John 1. 1–18 ct	W	CEG of Christmas	Jonah ch. 1 Col. 1. 1–14	Isa. 57. 15–end John 1. 1–18 ct
Ps. 132 Isa. 49. 7–13 Phil. 2. 1–11 Gospel: Luke 2. 41–52	W	**THE SUNDAY AFTER CHRISTMAS DAY** Isa. 62. 10–12 Ps. 45. 1–7 Gal. 4. 1–7 Matt. 1. 18–end	Ps. 105. 1–11 Isa. 35. 1–6 Gal. 3. 23–end	Ps. 132 Isa. 49. 7–13 Phil. 2. 1–11
Ps. **90**; 148 Isa. 59. 15b–end John 1. 29–34 or First EP of The Naming of Jesus Ps. 148 Jer. 23. 1–6 Col. 2. 8–15 ct	W	**Silvester, Bishop of Rome, 335** Com. Bishop	Jonah chs 3–4 Col. 1.24 – 2.7	Isa. 59. 15b–end John 1. 29–34 or First EP of The Circumcision of Christ (Ps. 148) Jer. 23. 1–6 Col. 2. 8–15 ct

January 2008

			Sunday Principal Service / Weekday Eucharist	Third Service / Morning Prayer
1	Tu	**THE NAMING AND CIRCUMCISION OF JESUS**	Num. 6. 22–end Ps. 8 Gal. 4. 4–7 Luke 2. 15–21	*MP*: Ps. *103*; 150 Gen. 17. 1–13 Rom. 2. 17–end
	W			
2	W	**Basil the Great and Gregory of Nazianzus, Bishops, Teachers, 379 and 389** *Seraphim, Monk of Sarov, Spiritual Guide, 1833; Vedanayagam Samuel Azariah, Bishop in South India, Evangelist, 1945* Com. Teacher *esp.* 2 Tim. 4. 1–8	or 1 John 2. 22–28 Ps. 98. 1–4	Ps. 18. 1–30 Ruth ch. 1
	W	Matt. 5. 13–19	John 1. 19–28	Col. 2. 8–end
3	Th		1 John 2.29 – 3.6 Ps. 98. 2–7	Ps. *127*; 128; 131 Ruth ch. 2
	W		John 1. 29–34	Col. 3. 1–11
4	F		1 John 3. 7–10 Ps. 98. 1, 8–end	Ps. 89. 1–37 Ruth ch. 3
	W		John 1. 35–42	Col 3.12 – 4.1
5	Sa		1 John 3. 11–21 Ps. 100 John 1. 43–end	Ps. 8; *48* Ruth 4. 1–17 Col. 4. 2–end
	W			
6	S	**THE EPIPHANY**	Isa. 60. 1–6 Ps. 72. [1–9] 10–15 Eph. 3. 1–12	*MP*: Ps. *132*; 113 Jer. 31. 7–14 John 1. 29–34
	W		Matt. 2. 1–12	
7	M		1 John 3.22 – 4.6 Ps. 2. 7–end Matt. 4. 12–17, 23–end	Ps. *99*; 147. 1–12 *alt.* Ps. 71 Baruch 1.15 – 2.10 *or* Jer. 23. 1–8
	W			Matt. 20. 1–16
8	Tu		1 John 4. 7–10 Ps. 72. 1–8 Mark 6. 34–44	Ps. *46*; 147. 13–end *alt.* Ps. 73 Baruch 2. 11–end *or* Jer. 30. 1–17
	W			Matt. 20. 17–28
9	W		1 John 4. 11–18 Ps. 72. 1, 10–13 Mark 6. 45–52	Ps. 2; *148* *alt.* Ps. 77 Baruch 3. 1–8 *or* Jer. 30.18 – 31.9
	W			Matt. 20. 29–end
10	Th	*William Laud, Archbishop of Canterbury, 1645* 	1 John 4.19 – 5.4 Ps. 72. 1, 17–end Luke 4. 14–22	Ps. 97; *149* *alt.* Ps. 78. 1–39† Baruch 3.9 – 4.4 *or* Jer. 31. 10–17
	W			Matt. 23. 1–12
11	F	*Mary Slessor, Missionary in West Africa, 1915* 	1 John 5. 5–13 Ps. 147. 13–end Luke 5. 12–16	Ps. 98; *150* *alt.* Ps. 55 Baruch 4. 21–30 *or* Jer. 33. 14–end
	W			Matt. 23. 13–28

BOOK OF COMMON PRAYER

Second Service Evening Prayer	Calendar and Holy Communion	Morning Prayer	Evening Prayer
EP: Ps. 115 Deut. 30. [1–10] 11–end Acts 3. 1–16	**THE CIRCUMCISION OF CHRIST** Additional collect Gen. 17. 3b–10 Ps. 98 Rom. 4. 8–13 *or* Eph. 2. 11–18 **W** Luke 2. 15–21	Ps. 103; 150 Gen. 17. 1–13 Rom. 2. 17–end	Ps. 115 Deut. 30. [1–10] 11–end Acts 3. 1–16
Ps. 45; **46** Isa. 60. 1–12 John 1. 35–42	**W**	Ruth ch. 1 Col. 2. 8–end	Isa. 60. 1–12 John 1. 35–42
Ps. **2**; 110 Isa. 60. 13–end John 1. 43–end	**W**	Ruth ch. 2 Col. 3. 1–11	Isa. 60. 13–end John 1. 43–end
Ps. 85; **87** Isa. ch. 61 John 2. 1–12	**W**	Ruth ch. 3 Col 3.12 – 4.1	Isa. ch. 61 John 2. 1–12
First EP of The Epiphany Ps. 96; **97** Isa. 49. 1–13 John 4. 7–26 ℣ ct	**W**	Ruth 4. 1–17 Col. 4. 2–end	*First EP of The Epiphany* Ps. 96; **97** Isa. 49. 1–13 John 4. 7–26 ℣ ct
EP: Ps. **98**; 100 Baruch 4.36 – 5.end *or* Isa. 60. 1–9 John 2. 1–11	**THE EPIPHANY** Isa. 60. 1–9 Ps. 100 Eph. 3. 1–12 ℣ Matt. 2. 1–12	Ps. 132; 113 Jer. 31. 7–14 John 1. 29–34	Ps. 72; 98 Baruch 4.36 – 5.end *or* Isa. 60. 1–9 John 2. 1–11
Ps. 118 *alt.* Ps. **72**; 75 Isa. 63. 7–end 1 John ch. 3	**W** *or* **G**	Baruch 1.15 – 2.10 *or* Jer. 23. 1–8 Matt. 20. 1–16	Isa. 63. 7–end 1 John ch. 3
Ps. 145 *alt.* Ps. 74 Isa. ch. 64 1 John 4. 7–end	**Lucian, Priest and Martyr, 290** Com. Martyr **Wr** *or* **Gr**	Baruch 2. 11–end *or* Jer. 30. 1–17 Matt. 20. 17–28	Isa. ch. 64 1 John 4. 7–end
Ps. **67**; 72 *alt.* Ps. 119. 81–104 Isa. 65. 1–16 1 John 5. 1–12	**W** *or* **G**	Baruch 3. 1–8 *or* Jer. 30.18 – 31.9 Matt. 20. 29–end	Isa. 65. 1–16 1 John 5. 1–12
Ps. 27; **29** *alt.* Ps. 78. 40–end† Isa. 65. 17–end 1 John 5. 13–end	**W** *or* **G**	Baruch 3.9 – 4.4 *or* Jer. 31. 10–17 Matt. 23. 1–12	Isa. 65. 17–end 1 John 5. 13–end
Ps. 93; 132 *alt.* Ps. 69 Isa. 66. 1–11 2 John	**W** *or* **G**	Baruch 4. 21–30 *or* Jer. 33. 14–end Matt. 23. 13–28	Isa. 66. 1–11 2 John

January 2008

Sunday Principal Service / Weekday Eucharist — *Third Service / Morning Prayer*

12 Sa **Aelred of Hexham, Abbot of Rievaulx, 1167**
Benedict Biscop, Abbot of Wearmouth, Scholar, 689
Com. Religious   *or*   1 John 5. 14–end
also Ecclus. 15. 1–6   Ps. 149. 1–5
                                John 3. 22–30

Ps. **96**; 145
alt. Ps. **76**; 79
Baruch 4. 36 – 5.end
or Mic. 5. 2–end
Matt. 23. 29–end

W

13 S **THE BAPTISM OF CHRIST**

Isa. 42. 1–9
Ps. 29
Acts 10. 34–43
Matt. 3. 13–end

Ps. 89. 19–29
Exod. 14. 15–22
1 John 5. 6–9

W

14 M
DEL 1
1 Sam. 1. 1–8
Ps. 116. 10–15
Mark 1. 14–20

Ps. **2**; 110
alt. **80**; 82
Gen. 1. 1–19
Matt. 21. 1–17

W

15 Tu
1 Sam. 1. 9–20
Canticle: 1 Sam. 2. 1, 4–8
or Magnificat
Mark 1. 21–28

Ps. 8; **9**
alt. Ps. 87; **89. 1–18**
Gen. 1.20 – 2.3
Matt. 21. 18–32

W

16 W
1 Sam. 3. 1–10, 19–20
Ps. 40. 1–4, 7–10
Mark 1. 29–39

Ps. 19; **20**
alt. Ps. 119. 105–128
Gen. 2. 4–end
Matt. 21. 33–end

W

17 Th **Antony of Egypt, Hermit, Abbot, 356**
Charles Gore, Bishop, Founder of the Community of the Resurrection, 1932
Com. Religious   *or*   1 Sam. 4. 1–11
esp. Phil. 3. 7–14   Ps. 44. 10–15, 24–25
also Matt. 19. 16–26   Mark 1. 40–end

Ps. **21**; 24
alt. Ps. 90; **92**
Gen. ch. 3
Matt. 22. 1–14

W

18 F The Week of Prayer for Christian Unity until 25th
1 Sam. 8. 4–7, 10–end
Ps. 89. 15–18
Mark 2. 1–12

Ps. **67**; 72
alt. Ps. **88**; (95)
Gen. 4. 1–16, 25–26
Matt. 22. 15–33

W

19 Sa **Wulfstan, Bishop of Worcester, 1095**
Com. Bishop   *or*   1 Sam. 9. 1–4, 17–19; 10. 1
esp. Matt. 24. 42–46   Ps. 21. 1–6
                            Mark 2. 13–17

Ps. 29; **33**
alt. Ps. 96; **97**; 100
Gen. 6. 1–10
Matt. 22. 34–end

W

20 S **THE THIRD SUNDAY OF EPIPHANY**

Isa. 49. 1–7
Ps. 40. 1–12
1 Cor. 1. 1–9
John 1. 29–42

Ps. 145. 1–12
Jer. 1. 4–10
Mark 1. 14–20

W

21 M **Agnes, Child Martyr at Rome, 304**
DEL 2
Com. Martyr   *or*   1 Sam. 15. 16–23
also Rev. 7. 13–end   Ps. 50. 8–10, 16–17, 24
                          Mark 2. 18–22

Ps. 145; **146**
alt. Ps. **98**; 99; 101
Gen. 6.11 – 7.10
Matt. 24. 1–14

Wr

BOOK OF COMMON PRAYER

Second Service Evening Prayer	Calendar and Holy Communion	Morning Prayer	Evening Prayer
Ps. **66**; 110 alt. Ps. 81; **84** Isa. 66. 12–23 3 John ct or First EP of The Baptism of Christ Ps. 36 Isa. ch. 61 Titus 2. 11–14; 3. 4–7 ℣ ct	W or G	Baruch 4.36 – 5.end or Mic. 5. 2–end Matt. 23. 29–end	Isa. 66. 12–23 3 John ct
Ps. 46; 47 Josh 3. 1–8, 14–end Heb. 1. 1–12 Gospel: Luke 3. 15–22	**THE FIRST SUNDAY AFTER EPIPHANY** To celebrate the Baptism of Christ, see *Common Worship* provision. Zechariah 8. 1–8 Ps. 72. 1–8 Rom. 12. 1–5 Luke 2. 41–end W or G	Ps. 89. 19–29 Exod. 14. 15–22 1 John 5. 6–9	Ps. 46; 47 Josh. 3. 1–8, 14–end Heb. 1. 1–12
Ps. **34**; 36 alt. Ps. **85**; 86 Amos ch. 1 1 Cor. 1. 1–17	W or G	Gen. 1. 1–19 Matt. 21. 1–17	Amos ch. 1 1 Cor. 1. 1–17
Ps. **45**; 46 alt. Ps. 89. 19–end Amos ch. 2 1 Cor. 1. 18–end	W or G	Gen. 1.20 – 2.3 Matt. 21. 18–32	Amos ch. 2 1 Cor. 1. 18–end
Ps. **47**; 48 alt. Ps. **91**; 93 Amos ch. 3 1 Cor. ch. 2	W or G	Gen. 2. 4–end Matt. 21. 33–end	Amos ch. 3 1 Cor. ch. 2
Ps. **61**; 65 alt. Ps. 94 Amos ch. 4 1 Cor. ch. 3	W or G	Gen. ch. 3 Matt. 22. 1–14	Amos ch. 4 1 Cor. ch. 3
Ps. 68 alt. Ps. 102 Amos 5. 1–17 1 Cor. ch. 4	**Prisca, Martyr at Rome, c. 265** Com. Virgin Martyr Wr or Gr	Gen. 4. 1–16, 25–26 Matt. 22. 15–33	Amos 5. 1–17 1 Cor. ch. 4
Ps. 84; **85** alt. Ps. 104 Amos 5. 18–end 1 Cor. ch. 5 ct	W or G	Gen. 6. 1–10 Matt. 22. 34–end	Amos 5. 18–end 1 Cor. ch. 5 ct
Ps. 96 Ezek. 2.1 – 3.4 Gal. 1. 11–end Gospel: John 1. 43–end	**SEPTUAGESIMA** Gen. 1. 1–5 Ps. 9. 10–20 1 Cor. 9. 24–end Matt. 20. 1–16 W or G	Ps. 145. 1–12 Jer. 1. 4–10 Mark 1. 14–20	Ps. 96 Ezek. 2.1 – 3.4 Gal. 1. 11–end
Ps. 71 alt. Ps. 105† (or Ps. 103) Amos ch. 6 1 Cor. 6. 1–11	**Agnes, Child Martyr at Rome, 304** Com. Virgin Martyr Wr or Gr	Gen. 6.11 – 7.10 Matt. 24. 1–14	Amos ch. 6 1 Cor. 6. 1–11

January 2008

			Sunday Principal Service / Weekday Eucharist	Third Service / Morning Prayer

22 Tu — Vincent of Saragossa, Deacon, first Martyr of Spain, 304
- 1 Sam. 16. 1–13
- Ps. 89. 19–27
- Mark 2. 23–end

Ps. *132*; 147. 1–12
alt. Ps. 106† (*or* Ps. 103)
Gen. 7. 11–end

W
Matt. 24. 15–28

23 W
- 1 Sam. 17. 32–33, 37, 40–51
- Ps. 144. 1–2, 9–10
- Mark 3. 1–6

Ps. *81*; 147. 13–end
alt. Ps. 110; *111*; 112
Gen. 8. 1–14

W
Matt. 24. 29–end

24 Th — Francis de Sales, Bishop of Geneva, Teacher, 1622
Com. Teacher   *or*   1 Sam. 18. 6–9; 19. 1–7
also Prov. 3. 13–18   Ps. 56. 1–2, 8–end
John 3. 17–21   Mark 3. 7–12

Ps. *76*; 148
alt. Ps. 113; *115*
Gen. 8.15 – 9.7
Matt. 25. 1–13

W

25 F — **THE CONVERSION OF PAUL**
The reading from Acts must be used as either the first or second reading at the Eucharist.
- Jer. 1. 4–10
- *or* Acts 9. 1–22
- Ps. 67
- Acts 9. 1–22
- *or* Gal. 1. 11–16a

MP: Ps. 66; 147. 13–end
Ezek. 3. 22–end
Phil. 3. 1–14

W
Matt. 19. 27–end

26 Sa — Timothy and Titus, Companions of Paul
- Isa. 61. 1–3a   *or*   2 Sam. 1. 1–4, 11–12, 17–19, 23–end
- Ps. 100   Ps. 80. 1–6
- 2 Tim. 2. 1–8   Mark 3. 20–21
- *or* Titus 1. 1–5

Ps. *122*; 128; 150
alt. Ps. 120; *121*; 122
Gen. 11. 1–9
Matt. 25. 31–end

W   Luke 10. 1–9

27 S — **THE FOURTH SUNDAY OF EPIPHANY**
- Isa. 9. 1–4
- Ps. 27. 1, 4–12 (*or* Ps. 27. 1–11)
- 1 Cor. 1. 10–18
- Matt. 4. 12–23

Ps. 113
Amos 3. 1–8
1 John 1. 1–4

W

28 M — Thomas Aquinas, Priest, Philosopher, Teacher, 1274
DEL 3
Com. Teacher   *or*   2 Sam. 5. 1–7, 10
esp. Wisd. 7. 7–10, 15–16   Ps. 89. 19–27
1 Cor. 2. 9–end   Mark 3. 22–30

Ps. 40; *108*
alt. Ps. 123; 124; 125; *126*
Gen. 11.27 – 12.9

W   John 16. 12–15
Matt. 26. 1–16

29 Tu
- 2 Sam. 6. 12–15, 17–19
- Ps. 24. 7–end
- Mark 3. 31–end

Ps. 34; *36*
alt. Ps. *132*; 133
Gen. 13. 2–end

W
Matt. 26. 17–35

30 W — Charles, King and Martyr, 1649
Com. Martyr   *or*   2 Sam. 7. 4–17
also Ecclus. 2. 12–17   Ps. 89. 19–27
1 Tim. 6. 12–16   Mark 4. 1–20

Ps. 45; *46*
alt. Ps. 119. 153–end
Gen. ch. 14

Wr
Matt. 26. 36–46

31 Th — John Bosco, Priest, Founder of the Salesian Teaching Order, 1888
- 2 Sam. 7. 18–19, 24–end
- Ps. 132. 1–5, 11–15
- Mark 4. 21–25

Ps. *47*; 48
alt. Ps. *143*; 146
Gen. ch. 15

W
Matt. 26. 47–56

BOOK OF COMMON PRAYER

Second Service Evening Prayer	Calendar and Holy Communion	Morning Prayer	Evening Prayer
	Vincent of Saragossa, Deacon, first Martyr of Spain, 304		
Ps. 89. 1–37 alt. Ps. 107† Amos ch. 7 1 Cor. 6. 12–end	Com. Martyr Wr or Gr	Gen. 7. 11–end Matt. 24. 15–28	Amos ch. 7 1 Cor. 6. 12–end
Ps. *97*; 98 alt. Ps. 119. 129–152 Amos ch. 8 1 Cor. 7. 1–24	W or G	Gen. 8. 1–14 Matt. 24. 29–end	Amos ch. 8 1 Cor. 7. 1–24
Ps. 99; 100; *111* alt. Ps. 114; *116*; 117 Amos ch. 9 1 Cor. 7. 25–end or First EP of The Conversion of Paul Ps. 149 Isa. 49. 1–13 Acts 22. 3–16 ct	W or G	Gen. 8.15 – 9.7 Matt. 25. 1–13	Amos ch. 9 1 Cor. 7. 25–end or First EP of The Conversion of Paul (Ps. 149) Isa. 49. 1–13 Acts 22. 3–16 W ct
	THE CONVERSION OF PAUL		
EP: Ps. 119. 41–56 Ecclus. 39. 1–10 or Isa. 56. 1–8 Col. 1.24 – 2.7	Josh. 5. 13–end Ps. 67 Acts 9. 1–22 Matt. 19. 27–end W	(Ps. 66; 147. 13–end) Ezek. 3. 22–end Phil. 3. 1–14	(Ps. 119. 41–56) Ecclus. 39. 1–10 or Isa. 56. 1–8 Col. 1.24 – 2.7
Ps. *61*; 66 alt. Ps. 118 Hos. 2. 2–17 1 Cor. 9. 1–14 ct	W or G	Gen. 11. 1–9 Matt. 25. 31–end	Hos. 2. 2–17 1 Cor. 9. 1–14 ct
	SEXAGESIMA		
Ps. 33. 1–12 [13–end] Eccles. 3. 1–11 1 Pet. 1. 3–12 Gospel: Luke 4. 14–21	Gen. 3. 9–19 Ps. 83. 1–2, 13–end 2 Cor. 11. 19–31 Luke 8. 4–15 W or G	Ps. 113 Amos 3. 1–8 1 John 1. 1–4	Ps. 33. 1–12 [13–end] Eccles. 3. 1–11 1 Pet. 1. 3–12
Ps. *138*; 144 alt. Ps. *127*; 128; 129 Hos. 2.18 – 3.end 1 Cor. 9. 15–end	W or G	Gen. 11.27 – 12.9 Matt. 26. 1–16	Hos. 2.18 – 3.end 1 Cor. 9. 15–end
Ps. 145 alt. Ps. (134); *135* Hos. 4. 1–16 1 Cor. 10. 1–13	W or G	Gen. 13. 2–end Matt. 26. 17–35	Hos. 4. 1–16 1 Cor. 10. 1–13
	Charles, King and Martyr, 1649		
Ps. 21; *29* alt. Ps. 136 Hos. 5. 1–7 1 Cor. 10.14 – 11.1	Com. Martyr Wr or Gr	Gen. ch. 14 Matt. 26. 36–46	Hos. 5. 1–7 1 Cor. 10.14 – 11.1
Ps. *24*; 33 alt. Ps. *138*; 140; 141 Hos. 5.8 – 6.6 1 Cor. 11. 2–16	W or G	Gen. ch. 15 Matt. 26. 47–56	Hos. 5.8 – 6.6 1 Cor. 11. 2–16

February 2008

			Sunday Principal Service / Weekday Eucharist	Third Service / Morning Prayer
1	F	Brigid, Abbess of Kildare, c. 525	2 Sam. 11. 1–10, 13–17 Ps. 51. 1–6, 9 Mark 4. 26–34	Ps. 61; **65** alt. Ps. 142; **144** Gen. ch. 16 Matt. 26. 57–end
2	W Sa	**THE PRESENTATION OF CHRIST IN THE TEMPLE (CANDLEMAS)** Mal. 3. 1–5 Ps. 24. [1–6] 7–end Heb. 2. 14–end Luke 2. 22–40	MP: Ps. **48**; 146 Exod. 13. 1–16 Rom. 12. 1–5
		or, if The Presentation is observed on 3 February: 2 Sam. 12. 1–7, 10–17 Ps. 51. 11–16 Mark 4. 35–end	Ps. 68 alt. Ps. 147 Gen. 17. 1–22 Matt. 27. 1–10
	G			
3	S G	THE SUNDAY NEXT BEFORE LENT	Exod. 24. 12–end Ps. 2 or Ps. 99 2 Pet. 1. 16–end Matt. 17. 1–9	Ps. 72 Exod. 34. 29–end 2 Cor. 4. 3–6
4 DEL 5	M G	Gilbert of Sempringham, Founder of the Gilbertine Order, 1189 Ordinary Time starts today 1 Kings 8. 1–7, 9–13 Ps. 132. 1–9 Mark 6. 53–end	Ps. **1**; 2; 3 Gen. 37. 1–11 Gal. ch. 1
5	Tu G		1 Kings 8. 22–23, 27–30 Ps. 84. 1–10 Mark 7. 1–13	Ps. **5**; 6; (8) Gen. 37. 12–end Gal. 2. 1–10
6	W P	**ASH WEDNESDAY** (The Accession of Queen Elizabeth II, 1952) Joel 2. 1–2, 12–17 or Isa. 58. 1–12 Ps. 51. 1–18 2 Cor. 5.20b – 6.10 Matt. 6. 1–6, 16–21 or John 8. 1–11	MP: Ps. 38 Dan. 9. 3–6, 17–19 1 Tim. 6. 6–19
7	Th P		Deut. 30. 15–end Ps. 1 Luke 9. 22–25	Ps. 77 alt. Ps. 14; **15**; 16 Gen. ch. 39 Gal. 2. 11–end
8	F P		Isa. 58. 1–9a Ps. 51. 1–5, 17–18 Matt. 9. 14–15	Ps. **3**; 7 alt. Ps. 17; **19** Gen. ch. 40 Gal. 3. 1–14

BOOK OF COMMON PRAYER 27

Second Service Evening Prayer	Calendar and Holy Communion	Morning Prayer	Evening Prayer
First EP of The Presentation Ps. 118 1 Sam. 1. 19b–end Heb. 4. 11–end ℣ ct *or, if The Presentation is kept on 3 Feb.:* Ps. **67**; 77 *alt.* Ps. 145 Hos. 6.7 – 7.2 1 Cor. 11. 17–end	W *or* G	Gen. ch. 16 Matt. 26. 57–end	*First EP of The Presentation* Ps. 118 1 Sam. 1. 19b–end Heb. 4. 11–end ℣ ct
EP: Ps. 122; **132** Hag. 2. 1–9 John 2. 18–22 Ps. 118 1 Sam. 1. 19b–end Heb. 4. 11–end ℣ ct	**THE PRESENTATION OF CHRIST IN THE TEMPLE** Mal. 3. 1–5 Ps. 48. 1–7 Gal. 4. 1–7 Luke 2. 22–40 ℣	Ps. 48; 146 Exod. 13. 1–16 Rom. 12. 1–5	Ps. 122; 132 Hag. 2. 1–9 John 2. 18–22
Ps. 84 Ecclus. 48. 1–10 *or* 2 Kings 2. 1–12 Matt. 17. [1–8] 9–23	**QUINQUAGESIMA** Gen. 9. 8–17 Ps. 77. 11–end 1 Cor. ch. 13 Luke 18. 31–43 G	Ps. 72 Exod. 34. 29–end 2 Cor. 4. 3–6	Ps. 84 Ecclus. 48. 1–10 *or* 2 Kings 2. 1–12 Matt. 17. [1–8] 9–23
Ps. **4**; 7 Jer. ch. 1 John 3. 1–21	G	Gen. 37. 1–11 Gal. ch. 1	Jer. ch. 1 John 3. 1–21
Ps. **9**; 10† Jer. 2. 1–13 John 3. 22–end	**Agatha, Martyr in Sicily, 251** Com. Virgin Martyr Gr	Gen. 37. 12–end Gal. 2. 1–10	Jer. 2. 1–13 John 3. 22–end
EP: Ps. **51** *or* Ps. 102. 1–18 [19–end] Isa. 1. 10–18 Luke 15. 11–end	**ASH WEDNESDAY** (The Accession of Queen Elizabeth II, 1952) Ash Wed. Coll. until 22 March Commination Joel 2. 12–17 Ps. 57 James 4. 1–10 Matt. 6. 16–21 P	Ps. 38 Dan. 9. 3–6, 17–19 1 Tim. 6. 6–19	Ps. 51 *or* Ps. 102. 1–18 [19–end] Isa. 1. 10–18 Luke 15. 11–end
Ps. 74 *alt.* Ps. 18† Jer. 2. 14–32 John 4. 1–26	Exod. 24. 12–end Matt. 8. 5–13 P	Gen. ch. 39 Gal. 2. 11–end	Jer. 2. 14–32 John 4. 1–26
Ps. 31 *alt.* Ps. 22 Jer. 3. 6–22 John 4. 27–42	1 Kings 19. 3b–8 Matt. 5.43 – 6.6 P	Gen. ch. 40 Gal. 3. 1–14	Jer. 3. 6–22 John 4. 27–42

February 2008

			Sunday Principal Service / Weekday Eucharist	Third Service / Morning Prayer
9	Sa		Isa. 58. 9b–end Ps. 86. 1–7 Luke 5. 27–32	Ps. 71 alt. Ps. 20; 21; **23** Gen. 41. 1–24 Gal. 3. 15–22
	P			
10	S	THE FIRST SUNDAY OF LENT	Gen. 2. 15–17; 3. 1–7 Ps. 32 Rom. 5. 12–19 Matt. 4. 1–11	Ps. 119. 1–16 Jer. 18. 1–11 Luke 18. 9–14
	P			
11	M		Lev. 19. 1–2, 11–18 Ps. 19. 7–end Matt. 25. 31–end	Ps. 10; **11** alt. Ps. 27; **30** Gen. 41. 25 – 45 Gal. 3.23 – 4.7
	P			
12	Tu		Isa. 55. 10–11 Ps. 34. 4–6, 21–22 Matt. 6. 7–15	Ps. 44 alt. Ps. 32; **36** Gen. 41.46 – 42.5 Gal. 4. 8–20
	P			
13	W	Ember Day*	Jonah ch. 3 Ps. 51. 1–5, 17–18 Luke 11. 29–32	Ps. **6**; 17 alt. Ps. 34 Gen. 42. 6–17 Gal. 4.21 – 5.1
	P			
14	Th	**Cyril and Methodius, Missionaries to the Slavs, 869 and 885** Valentine, Martyr at Rome, c. 269 Com. Missionaries *or* *esp.* Isa. 52. 7–10 *also* Rom. 10. 11–15	*or* Esther 14. 1–5, 12–14 *or* Isa. 55. 6–9 Ps. 138 Matt. 7. 7–12	Ps. **42**; 43 alt. Ps. 37† Gen. 42. 18–28 Gal. 5. 2–15
	Pw			
15	F	Ember Day* Sigfrid, Bishop, Apostle of Sweden, 1045; Thomas Bray, Priest, Founder of the SPCK and the SPG, 1730	Ezek. 18. 21–28 Ps. 130 Matt. 5. 20–26	Ps. 22 alt. Ps. 31 Gen. 42. 29–end Gal. 5. 16–end
	P			
16	Sa	Ember Day*	Deut. 26. 16–end Ps. 119. 1–8 Matt. 5. 43–end	Ps. 59; **63** alt. Ps. 41; **42**; 43 Gen. 43. 1–15 Gal. ch. 6
	P			
17	S	THE SECOND SUNDAY OF LENT	Gen. 12. 1–4a Ps. 121 Rom. 4. 1–5, 13–17 John 3. 1–17	Ps. 74 Jer. 22. 1–9 Matt. 8. 1–13
	P			
18	M		Dan. 9. 4–10 Ps. 79. 8–9, 12, 14 Luke 6. 36–38	Ps. 26; **32** alt. Ps. 44 Gen. 43. 16–end Heb. ch. 1
	P			
19	Tu		Isa. 1. 10, 16–20 Ps. 50. 8, 16–end Matt. 23. 1–12	Ps. 50 alt. Ps. **48**; 52 Gen. 44. 1–17 Heb. 2. 1–9
	P			

*For Ember Day provision, see p. 13.

BOOK OF COMMON PRAYER

Second Service Evening Prayer	Calendar and Holy Communion	Morning Prayer	Evening Prayer
Ps. 73 alt. Ps. **24**; 25 Jer. 4. 1–18 John 4. 43–end ct	Isa. 38. 1–6a Mark 6. 45–end P	Gen. 41. 1–24 Gal. 3. 15–22	Jer. 4. 1–18 John 4. 43–end ct
Ps. 50. 1–15 Deut. 6. 4–9, 16–end Luke 15. 1–10	**THE FIRST SUNDAY IN LENT** Coll. (1) Lent 1 (2) Ash Wednesday Ember until 16 Feb. Gen. 3. 1–6 Ps. 91. 1–12 2 Cor. 6. 1–10 Matt. 4. 1–11 P	Ps. 119. 1–16 Jer. 18. 1–11 Luke 18. 9–14	Ps. 50. 1–15 Deut. 6. 4–9, 16–end Luke 15. 1–10
Ps. 12; **13**; 14 alt. Ps. 26; **28**; 29 Jer. 4. 19–end John 5. 1–18	Ezek. 34. 11–16a Matt. 25. 31–end P	Gen. 41. 25–45 Gal. 3.23 – 4.7	Jer. 4. 19–end John 5. 1–18
Ps. 46; **49** alt. Ps. 33 Jer. 5. 1–19 John 5. 19–29	Isa. 55. 6–11 Matt. 21. 10–16 P	Gen. 41.46 – 42.5 Gal. 4. 8–20	Jer. 5. 1–19 John 5. 19–29
Ps. 9; **28** alt. Ps. 119. 33–56 Jer. 5. 20–end John 5. 30–end	Ember Day Ember CEG or Isa. 58. 1–9a Matt. 12. 38–end P	Gen. 42. 6–17 Gal. 4.21 – 5.1	Jer. 5. 20–end John 5. 30–end
	Valentine, Martyr at Rome, c. 269		
Ps. 137; 138; **142** alt. Ps. 39; **40** Jer. 6. 9–21 John 6. 1–15	Com. Martyr or Isa. 58. 9b–end John 8. 31–45 Pr	Gen. 42. 18–28 Gal. 5. 2–15	Jer. 6. 9–21 John 6. 1–15
Ps. 54; **55** alt. Ps. 35 Jer. 6. 22–end John 6. 16–27	Ember Day Ember CEG or Ezek. 18. 20–25 John 5. 2–15 P	Gen. 42. 29–end Gal. 5. 16–end	Jer. 6. 22–end John 6. 16–27
Ps. **4**; 16 alt. Ps. 45; **46** Jer. 7. 1–20 John 6. 27–40 ct	Ember Day Ember CEG or Ezek. 18. 26–end Matt. 17. 1–9 or Luke 4. 16–21 or John 10. 1–16 P	Gen. 43. 1–15 Gal. ch. 6	Jer. 7. 1–20 John 6. 27–40 ct
Ps. 135. 1–14 [15–end] Num. 21. 4–9 Luke 14. 27–33	**THE SECOND SUNDAY IN LENT** Jer. 17. 5–10 Ps. 25. 13–end 1 Thess. 4. 1–8 Matt. 15. 21–28 P	Ps. 74 Jer. 22. 1–9 Matt. 8. 1–13	Ps. 135. 1–14 [15–end] Num. 21. 4–9 Luke 14. 27–33
Ps. 70; **74** alt. Ps. **47**; 49 Jer. 7. 21–end John 6. 41–51	Heb. 2. 1–10 John 8. 21–30 P	Gen. 43. 16–end Heb. ch. 1	Jer. 7. 21–end John 6. 41–51
Ps. **52**; 53; 54 alt. Ps. 50 Jer. 8. 1–15 John 6. 52–59	Heb. 2. 11–end Matt. 23. 1–12 P	Gen. 44. 1–17 Heb. 2. 1–9	Jer. 8. 1–15 John 6. 52–59

February 2008

			Sunday Principal Service / Weekday Eucharist	Third Service / Morning Prayer
20	W P		Jer. 18. 18–20 Ps. 31. 4–5, 14–18 Matt. 20. 17–28	Ps. 35 *alt.* Ps. 119. 57–80 Gen. 44. 18–end Heb. 2. 10–end
21	Th P		Jer. 17. 5–10 Ps. 1 Luke 16. 19–end	Ps. 34 *alt.* Ps. 56; **57**; (63†) Gen. 45. 1–15 Heb. 3. 1–6
22	F P		Gen. 37. 3–4, 12–13, 17–28 Ps. 105. 16–22 Matt. 21. 33–43, 45–46	Ps. 40; **41** *alt.* Ps. **51**; 54 Gen. 45. 16–end Heb. 3. 7–end
23	Sa Pr	**Polycarp, Bishop of Smyrna, Martyr, c. 155** Com. Martyr *or* *also* Rev. 2. 8–11	Mic. 7. 4–15, 18–20 Ps. 103. 1–4, 9–12 Luke 15. 1–3, 11–end	Ps. 3; **25** *alt.* Ps. 68 Gen. 46. 1–7, 28–end Heb. 4. 1–13
24	S P	THE THIRD SUNDAY OF LENT	Exod. 17. 1–7 Ps. 95 Rom. 5. 1–11 John 4. 5–42	Ps. 46 Amos 7. 10–end 2 Cor. 1. 1–11
25	M* ** P		2 Kings 5. 1–15 Ps. 42. 1–2; 43. 1–4 Luke 4. 24–30	Ps. **5**; 7 *alt.* Ps. 71 Gen. 47. 1–27 Heb. 4.14 – 5.10
26	Tu P		Song of the Three 2, 11–20 *or* Dan. 2. 20–23 Ps. 25. 3–10 Matt. 18. 21–25	Ps. 6; **9** *alt.* Ps. 73 Gen. 47.28 – 48.end Heb. 5.11 – 6.12
27	W Pw	**George Herbert, Priest, Poet, 1633** Com. Pastor *or* *esp.* Mal. 2. 5–7 Matt. 11. 25–end *also* Rev. 19. 5–9	Deut. 4. 1, 5–9 Ps. 147. 13–end Matt. 5. 17–19	Ps. 38 *alt.* Ps. 77 Gen. 49. 1–32 Heb. 6. 13–end
28	Th P		Jer. 7. 23–28 Ps. 95. 1–2, 6–end Luke 11. 14–23	Ps. **56**; 57 *alt.* Ps. 78. 1–39† Gen. 49.33 – 50.end Heb. 7. 1–10
29	F P		Hos. 14. 2–10 Ps. 81. 6–10, 13, 16 Mark 12. 28–34	Ps. 22 *alt.* Ps. 55 Exod. 1. 1–14 Heb. 7. 11–end

*Matthias may be celebrated on Monday 25 February instead of 14 May.
**The following readings may replace those provided for Holy Communion on any day during the Third Week of Lent: Exod. 17. 1–7; Ps. 95. 1–2, 6–end; John 4. 5–42.

BOOK OF COMMON PRAYER

Second Service Evening Prayer		Calendar and Holy Communion	Morning Prayer	Evening Prayer
Ps. *3*; 51 *alt.* Ps. *59*; 60 (67) Jer. 8.18 – 9.11 John 6. 60–end	P	Heb. 3. 1–6 Matt. 20. 17–28	Gen. 44. 18–end Heb. 2. 10–end	Jer. 8.18 – 9.11 John 6. 60–end
Ps. 71 *alt.* Ps. 61; *62*; 64 Jer. 9. 12–24 John 7. 1–13	P	Heb. 3. 7–end John 5. 30–end	Gen. 45. 1–15 Heb. 3. 1–6	Jer. 9. 12–24 John 7. 1–13
Ps. *6*; 38 *alt.* Ps. 38 Jer. 10. 1–16 John 7. 14–24	P	Heb. ch. 4 Matt. 21. 33–end	Gen. 45. 16–end Heb. 3. 7–end	Jer. 10. 1–16 John 7. 14–24
Ps. *23*; 27 *alt.* Ps. 65; *66* Jer. 10. 17–24 John 7. 25–36 ct	P	Heb. ch. 5 Luke 15. 11–end	Gen. 46. 1–7, 28–end Heb. 4. 1–13	Jer. 10. 17–24 John 7. 25–36 ct
Ps. 40 Josh. 1. 1–9 Eph. 6. 10–20 *Gospel:* John 2. 13–22	P	**THE THIRD SUNDAY IN LENT** Num. 22. 21–31 Ps. 9. 13–end Eph. 5. 1–14 Luke 11. 14–28	Ps. 46 Amos 7. 10–end 2 Cor. 1. 1–11	Ps. 40 Josh. 1. 1–9 Eph. 6. 10–20
Ps. 11; *17* *alt.* Ps. *72*; 75 Jer. 11. 1–17 John 7. 37–52	R	**MATTHIAS THE APOSTLE** (transferred from 24th) 1 Sam. 2. 27–35 Ps. 16. 1–7 Acts 1. 15–end Matt. 11. 25–end	(Ps. 15) Jonah 1. 1–9 Acts 2. 37–end	(Ps. 80) 1 Sam. 16. 1–13a Matt. 7. 15–27
Ps. 61; 62; *64* *alt.* Ps. 74 Jer. 11.18 – 12.6 John 7.53 – 8.11	P	Heb. 6. 11–end Matt. 18. 15–22	Gen. 47.28 – 48.end Heb. 5.11 – 6.12	Jer. 11.18 – 12.6 John 7.53 – 8.11
Ps. 36; *39* *alt.* Ps. 119. 81–104† Jer. 13. 1–11 John 8. 12–30	P	Heb. 7. 1–10 Matt. 15. 1–20	Gen. 49. 1–32 Heb. 6. 13–end	Jer. 13. 1–11 John 8. 12–30
Ps. *59*; 60 *alt.* Ps. 78. 40–end† Jer. ch. 14 John 8. 31–47	P	Heb. 7. 11–25 John 6. 26–35	Gen. 49.33 – 50.end Heb. 7. 1–10	Jer. ch. 14 John 8. 31–47
Ps. 69 *alt.* Ps. 69 Jer. 15. 10–end John 8. 48–end	P	Heb. 7. 26–end John 4. 5–26	Exod. 1. 1–14 Heb. 7. 11–end	Jer. 15. 10–end John 8. 48–end

March 2008

			Sunday Principal Service / Weekday Eucharist	Third Service / Morning Prayer
1	Sa	**David, Bishop of Menevia, Patron of Wales, c. 601** Com. Bishop *or* *also* 2 Sam. 23. 1–4 Ps. 89. 19–22, 24	Hos. 5.15 – 6.6 Ps. 51. 1–2, 17–end Luke 18. 9–14	Ps. 31 *alt.* Ps. **76**; 79 Exod. 1.22 – 2.10 Heb. ch. 8
	Pw			
2	S	**THE FOURTH SUNDAY OF LENT** (Mothering Sunday)	1 Sam. 16. 1–13 Ps. 23 Eph. 5. 8–14 John ch. 9	Ps. 19 Isa. 43. 1–7 Eph. 2. 8–14
		or, for Mothering Sunday:	Exod. 2. 1–10 *or* 1 Sam. 1. 20–end Ps. 34. 11–20 *or* Ps. 127. 1–4 2 Cor. 1. 3–7 *or* Col. 3. 12–17 Luke 2. 33–35 *or* John 19. 25b–27	
	P			
3	M*		Isa. 65. 17–21 Ps. 30. 1–5, 8, 11–end John 4. 43–end	Ps. 70; **77** *alt.* Ps. **80**; 82 Exod. 2. 11–22 Heb. 9. 1–14
	P			
4	Tu		Ezek. 47. 1–9, 12 Ps. 46. 1–8 John 5. 1–3, 5–16	Ps. 54; **79** *alt.* Ps. 87; **89**. **1–18** Exod. 2.23 – 3.20 Heb. 9. 15–end
	P			
5	W		Isa. 49. 8–15 Ps. 145. 8–18 John 5. 17–30	Ps. 63; **90** *alt.* Ps. 119. 105–128 Exod. 4. 1–23 Heb. 10. 1–18
	P			
6	Th		Exod. 32. 7–14 Ps. 106. 19–23 John 5. 31–47	Ps. 53; **86** *alt.* Ps. 90; **92** Exod. 4.27 – 6.1 Heb. 10. 19–25
	P			
7	F	**Perpetua, Felicity and their Companions, Martyrs at Carthage, 203** Com. Martyr *or* *esp.* Rev. 12. 10–12a *also* Wisd. 3. 1–7	Wisd. 2. 1, 12–22 *or* Jer. 26. 8–11 Ps. 34. 15–end John 7. 1–2, 10, 25–30	Ps. 102 *alt.* Ps. **88**; (95) Exod. 6. 2–13 Heb. 10. 26–end
	Pr			
8	Sa	**Edward King, Bishop of Lincoln, 1910** *Felix, Bishop, Apostle to the East Angles, 647; Geoffrey Studdert Kennedy, Priest, Poet, 1929* Com. Bishop *or* *also* Heb. 13. 1–8	Jer. 11. 18–20 Ps. 7. 1–2, 8–10 John 7. 40–52	Ps. 32 *alt.* Ps. 96; **97**; 100 Exod. 7. 8–end Heb. 11. 1–16
	Pw			
9	S	**THE FIFTH SUNDAY OF LENT (Passiontide begins)**	Ezek. 37. 1–14 Ps. 130 Rom. 8. 6–11 John 11. 1–45	Ps. 86 Jer. 31. 27–37 John 12. 20–33
	P			
10	M**		Susanna 1–9, 15–17, 19–30, 33–62 (*or* 41b–62) *or* Josh. 2. 1–14 Ps. 23 John 8. 1–11	Ps. **73**; 121 *alt.* Ps. **98**; 99; 101 Exod. 8. 1–19 Heb. 11. 17–31
	P			

*The following readings may replace those provided for Holy Communion on any day during the Fourth Week of Lent: Mic. 7. 7–9; Ps. 27. 1, 9–10, 16–17; John ch. 9.
**The following readings may replace those provided for Holy Communion on any day during the Fifth Week of Lent: 2 Kings 4. 18–21, 32–37; Ps. 17. 1–8, 16; John 11. 1–45.

BOOK OF COMMON PRAYER

Second Service Evening Prayer	Calendar and Holy Communion	Morning Prayer	Evening Prayer
Ps. *116*; 130 alt. Ps. 81; **84** Jer. 16.10 – 17.4 John 9. 1–17 ct	**David, Bishop of Menevia, Patron of Wales, c. 601** Com. Bishop *or* Heb. 8. 1–6 John 8. 1–11 Pw	Exod. 1.22 – 2.10 Heb. ch. 8	Jer. 16.10 – 17.4 John 9. 1–17 ct
Ps. 31. 1–8 [9–16] Mic. ch. 7 *or* Prayer of Manasseh James ch. 5 Gospel: John 3. 14–21 If the Principal Service readings for The Fourth Sunday of Lent are displaced by Mothering Sunday provisions, they may be used at the Second Service.	**THE FOURTH SUNDAY IN LENT** To celebrate Mothering Sunday, see *Common Worship* provision. Exod. 16. 2–7a Ps. 122 Gal. 4. 21–end *or* Heb. 12. 22–24 John 6. 1–14 P	Ps. 19 Isa. 43. 1–7 Eph. 2. 8–14	Ps. 31. 1–8 [9–16] Mic. ch. 7 *or* Prayer of Manasseh James ch. 5
Ps. *25*; 28 alt. Ps. **85**; 86 Jer. 17. 5–18 John 9. 18–end	Heb. 11. 1–6 John 2. 13–end P	Exod. 2. 11–22 Heb. 9. 1–14	Jer. 17. 5–18 John 9. 18–end
Ps. **80**; 82 alt. Ps. 89. 19–end Jer. 18. 1–12 John 10. 1–10	Heb. 11. 13–16a John 7. 14–24 P	Exod. 2.23 – 3.20 Heb. 9. 15–end	Jer. 18. 1–12 John 10. 1–10
Ps. 52; **91** alt. Ps. **91**; 93 Jer. 18. 13–end John 10. 11–21	Heb. 12. 1–11 John 9. 1–17 P	Exod. 4. 1–23 Heb. 10. 1–18	Jer. 18. 13–end John 10. 11–21
Ps. 94 alt. Ps. 94 Jer. 19. 1–13 John 10. 22–end	Heb. 12. 12–17 John 5. 17–27 P	Exod. 4.27 – 6.1 Heb. 10. 19–25	Jer. 19. 1–13 John 10. 22–end
Ps. 13; **16** alt. Ps. 102 Jer. 19.14 – 20.6 John 11. 1–16	**Perpetua, Felicity and their Companions, Martyrs at Carthage, 203** Com. Martyr *or* Heb. 12. 22–end John 11. 33–46 Pr	Exod. 6. 2–13 Heb. 10. 26–end	Jer. 19.14 – 20.6 John 11. 1–16
Ps. *140*; 141; 142 alt. Ps. 104 Jer. 20. 7–end John 11. 17–27 ct	Heb. 13. 7–21 John 8. 12–20 P	Exod. 7. 8–end Heb. 11. 1–16	Jer. 20. 7–end John 11. 17–27 ct
Ps. 30 Lam. 3. 19–33 Matt. 20. 17–end	**THE FIFTH SUNDAY IN LENT** Exod. 24. 4–8 Ps. 143 Heb. 9. 11–15 John 8. 46–end P	Ps. 86 Jer. 31. 27–37 John 12. 20–33	Ps. 30 Lam. 3. 19–33 Matt. 20. 17–end
Ps. **26**; 27 alt. Ps. **105**† (*or* 103) Jer. 21. 1–10 John 11. 28–44	Col. 1. 13–23a John 7. 1–13 P	Exod. 8. 1–19 Heb. 11. 17–31	Jer. 21. 1–10 John 11. 28–44

March 2008

			Sunday Principal Service / Weekday Eucharist	Third Service / Morning Prayer
11	Tu / P		Num. 21. 4–9 Ps. 102. 1–3, 16–23 John 8. 21–30	Ps. *35*; 123 *alt.* Ps. *106*† (or 103) Exod. 8. 20–end Heb. 11.32 – 12.2
12	W / P		Dan. 3. 14–20, 24–25, 28 *Canticle*: Bless the Lord John 8. 31–42	Ps. *55*; 124 *alt.* Ps. 110; *111*; 112 Exod. 9. 1–12 Heb. 12. 3–13
13	Th / P		Gen. 17. 3–9 Ps. 105. 4–9 John 8. 51–end	Ps. *40*; 125 *alt.* Ps. 113; *115* Exod. 9. 13–end Heb. 12. 14–end
14	F / P		Jer. 20. 10–13 Ps. 18. 1–6 John 10. 31–end	Ps. *22*; 126 *alt.* Ps. 139 Exod. ch. 10 Heb. 13. 1–16
15	Sa / P		Ezek. 37. 21–28 *Canticle*: Jer. 31. 10–13 *or* Ps. 121 John 11. 45–end	Ps. *23*; 127 *alt.* Ps. 120; *121*; 122 Exod. ch. 11 Heb. 13. 17–end
16	S / R	**PALM SUNDAY** *Liturgy of the Palms* Matt. 21. 1–11 Ps. 118. [1–2] 19–24 [25–end]	*Liturgy of the Passion* Isa. 50. 4–9a Ps. 31. 9–16 [17–18] Phil. 2. 5–11 Matt. 26.14 – 27.end *or* Matt. 27. 11–54	Ps. 61; 62 Zech. 9. 9–12 Luke 16. 19–end
17	M / R	**MONDAY OF HOLY WEEK**	Isa. 42. 1–9 Ps. 36. 5–11 Heb. 9. 11–15 John 12. 1–11	MP: Ps. 41 Lam. 1. 1–12a Luke 22. 1–23
18	Tu / R	**TUESDAY OF HOLY WEEK**	Isa. 49. 1–7 Ps. 71. 1–8 [9–14] 1 Cor. 1. 18–31 John 12. 20–36	MP: Ps. 27 Lam. 3. 1–18 Luke 22. [24–38] 39–53
19	W / R	**WEDNESDAY OF HOLY WEEK**	Isa. 50. 4–9a Ps. 70 Heb. 12. 1–3 John 13. 21–32	MP: Ps. 102. 1–17 [18–end] Wisd. 1.16 – 2.1, 12–22 *or* Jer. 11. 18–20 Luke 22. 54–end
20	Th / W (HC) R	**MAUNDY THURSDAY***	Exod. 12. 1–4 [5–10], 11–14 Ps. 116. 1, 10–end (*or* 9–end) 1 Cor. 11. 23–26 John 13. 1–17, 31b–35	MP: Ps. 42; 43 Lev. 16. 2–24 Luke 23. 1–25
21	F / R	**GOOD FRIDAY**	Isa. 52.13 – 53.end Ps. 22 (*or* 22. 1–11 *or* 22. 1–21) Heb. 10. 16–25 *or* Heb. 4. 14–16 John 18.1 – 19.end	MP: Ps. 69 Gen. 22. 1–18 A part of John chs 18 – 19 if not read at the Principal Service *or* Heb. 10. 1–10

*Cuthbert may be celebrated on 4 September instead of 20 March.

BOOK OF COMMON PRAYER

Second Service Evening Prayer	Calendar and Holy Communion	Morning Prayer	Evening Prayer
Ps. *61*; 64 alt. Ps. 107† Jer. 22. 1–5, 13–19 John 11. 45–end	Col. 2. 8–12 John 7. 32–39 P	Exod. 8. 20–end Heb. 11.32 – 12.2	Jer. 22. 1–5, 13–19 John 11. 45–end
Ps. 56; *62* alt. Ps. 119. 129–152 Jer. 22.20 – 23.8 John 12. 1–11	**Gregory the Great, Bishop of Rome, 604** Com. Doctor or Col. 2. 13–19 John 7. 40–end Pw	Exod. 9. 1–12 Heb. 12. 3–13	Jer. 22.20 – 23.8 John 12. 1–11
Ps. 42; *43* alt. Ps. 114; *116*; 117 Jer. 23. 9–32 John 12. 12–19	Col. 3. 8–11 John 10. 22–38 P	Exod. 9. 13–end Heb. 12. 14–end	Jer. 23. 9–32 John 12. 12–19
Ps. 31 alt. Ps. *130*; 131; 137 Jer. ch. 24 John 12. 20–36a	Col. 3. 12–17 John 11. 47–54 P	Exod. ch. 10 Heb. 13. 1–16	Jer. ch. 24 John 12. 20–36a
Ps. 128; 129; *130* alt. Ps. 118 Jer. 25. 1–14 John 12. 36b–end ct	Col. 4. 2–6 John 6. 53–end P	Exod. ch. 11 Heb. 13. 17–end	Jer. 25. 1–14 John 12. 36b–end ct
Ps. 80 Isa. 5. 1–7 Matt. 21. 33–end	**PALM SUNDAY** Zech. 9. 9–12 Ps. 73. 22–end Phil. 2. 5–11 Passion acc. to Matthew Matt. 27. 1–54 or Matt. 26.1 – 27.61 or Matt. 21. 1–13 R	Ps. 61; 62 Isa. 42. 1–9 Luke 16. 19–end	Ps. 80 Isa. 5. 1–7 Matt. 21. 33–end
EP: Ps. 25 Lam. 2. 8–19 Col. 1. 18–23	**MONDAY IN HOLY WEEK** Isa. 63. 1–19 Ps. 55. 1–8 Gal. 6. 1–11 Mark ch. 14 R	Ps. 41 Lam. 1. 1–12a John 12. 1–11	Ps. 25 Lam. 2. 8–19 Col. 1. 18–23
EP: Ps. 55. 13–24 Lam. 3. 40–51 Gal. 6. 11–end	**TUESDAY IN HOLY WEEK** Isa. 50. 5–11 Ps. 13 Rom. 5. 6–19 Mark 15. 1–39 R	Ps. 27 Lam. 3. 1–18 John 12. 20–36	Ps. 55. 13–24 Lam. 3. 40–51 Gal. 6. 11–end
EP: Ps. 88 Isa. 63. 1–9 Rev. 14.18 – 15.4	**WEDNESDAY IN HOLY WEEK** Isa. 49. 1–9a Ps. 54 Heb. 9. 16–end Luke ch. 22 R	Ps. 102. 1–17 [18–end] Wisd. 1.16 – 2.1, 12–22 or Jer. 11. 18–20 John 13. 21–32	Ps. 88 Isa. 63. 1–9 Rev. 14.18 – 15.4
EP: Ps. 39 Exod. ch. 11 Eph. 2. 11–18	**MAUNDY THURSDAY** Exod. 12. 1–11 Ps. 43 1 Cor. 11. 17–end Luke 23. 1–49 W (HC) R	Ps. 42; 43 Lev. 16. 2–24 John 13. 1–17, 31b–35	Ps. 39 Exod. ch. 11 Eph. 2. 11–18
EP: Ps. 130; 143 Lam. 5. 15–end A part of John 18 – 19 if not read at the Principal Service, especially John 19. 38–end or Col. 1. 18–23	**GOOD FRIDAY** Alt. Collect Passion acc. to John Alt. Gospel, if Passion is read Num. 21. 4–9 Ps. 140. 1–9 Heb. 10. 1–25 John 19. 1–37 or John 19. 38–end R	Ps. 69 Gen. 22. 1–18 John ch. 18	Ps. 130; 143 Lam. 5. 15–end John 19. 38–end

March 2008

			Sunday Principal Service / Weekday Eucharist	Third Service / Morning Prayer
22	Sa	**EASTER EVE** *These readings are for use at services other than the Easter Vigil*	Job 14. 1–14 *or* Lam. 3. 1–9, 19–24 Ps. 31. 1–4, 15–16 (*or* 1–5) 1 Pet. 4. 1–8 Matt. 27. 57–end *or* John 19. 38–end	Ps. 142 Hos. 6. 1–6 John 2. 18–22
23	S	**EASTER DAY** *The following readings and psalms (or canticles) are provided for use at the Easter Vigil. A minimum of three Old Testament readings should be chosen. The reading from Exodus ch. 14 should always be used.*	Gen. 1.1 – 2.4a & Ps. 136. 1–9, 23–end Gen. 7. 1–5, 11–18; 8. 6–18; 9. 8–13 & Ps. 46 Gen. 22. 1–18 & Ps. 16 Exod. 14. 10–end; 15. 20–21 & *Canticle*: Exod. 15. 1b–13, 17–18 Isa. 55. 1–11 & *Canticle*: Isa. 12. 2–end Baruch 3.9–15, 32 – 4.4 & Ps. 19 *or* Prov. 8. 1–8, 19–21; 9. 4b–6 & Ps. 19 Ezek. 36. 24–28 & Ps. 42; 43 Ezek. 37. 1–14 & Ps. 143 Zeph. 3. 14–end & Ps. 98 Rom. 6. 3–11 & Ps. 114 Matt. 28. 1–10	
		Easter Day Services *The reading from Acts must be used as either the first or second reading at the Principal Service*	Acts 10. 34–43 *or* Jer. 31. 1–6 Ps. 118. [1–2] 14–24 Col. 3. 1–4 *or* Acts 10. 34–43 John 20. 1–18 *or* Matt. 28. 1–10	MP: Ps. 114; 117 Exod. 14.10–18, 26 – 15.2 Rev. 15. 2–4
24	M W	**MONDAY OF EASTER WEEK**	Acts 2. 14, 22–32 Ps. 16. 1–2, 6–end Matt. 28. 8–15	Ps. *111*; 117; 146 Exod. 12. 1–14 1 Cor. 15. 1–11
25	Tu W	**TUESDAY OF EASTER WEEK**	Acts 2. 36–41 Ps. 33. 4–5, 18–end John 20. 11–18	Ps. *112*; 147. 1–12 Exod. 12. 14–36 1 Cor. 15. 12–19
26	W W	**WEDNESDAY OF EASTER WEEK**	Acts 3. 1–10 Ps. 105. 1–9 Luke 24. 13–35	Ps. *113*; 147. 13–end Exod. 12. 37–end 1 Cor. 15. 20–28
27	Th W	**THURSDAY OF EASTER WEEK**	Acts 3. 11–end Ps. 8 Luke 24. 35–48	Ps. *114*; 148 Exod. 13. 1–16 1 Cor. 15. 29–34
28	F W	**FRIDAY OF EASTER WEEK**	Acts 4. 1–12 Ps. 118. 1–4, 22–26 John 21. 1–14	Ps. *115*; 149 Exod. 13.17 – 14.14 1 Cor. 15. 35–50
29	Sa W	**SATURDAY OF EASTER WEEK**	Acts 4. 13–21 Ps. 118. 1–4, 14–21 Mark 16. 9–15	Ps. *116*; 150 Exod. 14. 15–end 1 Cor. 15. 51–end

BOOK OF COMMON PRAYER 37

Second Service Evening Prayer	Calendar and Holy Communion	Morning Prayer	Evening Prayer
Ps. 116 Job 19. 21–27 1 John 5. 5–12	**EASTER EVE** Job 14. 1–14 1 Pet. 3. 17–22 Matt. 27. 57–end	Ps. 142 Hos. 6. 1–6 John 2. 18–22	Ps. 116 Job 19. 21–27 1 John 5. 5–12
	EASTER DAY Exod. 12. 21–28 Ps. 111 Col. 3. 1–7 John 20. 1–10	Ps. 114; 117 Exod. 14. 10–18, 26 – 15.2 Rev. 15. 2–4	Ps. 105 or Ps. 66. 1–11 Song of Sol. 3. 2–5; 8. 6–7 John 20. 11–18 or Rev. 1. 12–18
EP: Ps. 105 or Ps. 66. 1–11 Song of Sol. 3. 2–5; 8. 6–7 John 20. 11–18 *if not used at the Principal Service* or Rev. 1. 12–18	⅏		
Ps. 135 Song of Sol. 1.9 – 2.7 Mark 16. 1–8	**MONDAY IN EASTER WEEK** Hos. 6. 1–6 Easter Anthems Acts 10. 34–43 W Luke 24. 13–35	Exod. 12. 1–14 1 Cor. 15. 1–11	Song of Sol. 1.9 – 2.7 Mark 16. 1–8
Ps. 136 Song of Sol. 2. 8–end Luke 24. 1–12	**TUESDAY IN EASTER WEEK** 1 Kings 17. 17–end Ps. 16. 9–end Acts 13. 26–41 W Luke 24. 36b–48	Exod. 12. 14–36 1 Cor. 15. 12–19	Song of Sol. 2. 8–end Luke 24. 1–12
Ps. 105 Song of Sol. ch. 3 Matt. 28. 16–end	**WEDNESDAY IN EASTER WEEK** Isa. 42. 10–16 Ps. 111 Acts 3. 12–18 W John 20. 11–18	Exod. 12. 37–end 1 Cor. 15. 20–28	Song of Sol. ch. 3 Matt. 28. 16–end
Ps. 106 Song of Sol. 5.2 – 6.3 Luke 7. 11–17	**THURSDAY IN EASTER WEEK** Isa. 43. 16–21 Ps. 113 Acts 8. 26–end W John 21. 1–14	Exod. 13. 1–16 1 Cor. 15. 29–34	Song of Sol. 5.2 – 6.3 Luke 7. 11–17
Ps. 107 Song of Sol. 7.10 – 8.4 Luke 8. 41–end	**FRIDAY IN EASTER WEEK** Ezek. 37. 1–14 Ps. 116. 1–9 1 Pet. 3. 18–end W Matt. 28. 16–end	Exod. 13.17 – 14.14 1 Cor. 15. 35–50	Song of Sol. 7.10 – 8.4 Luke 8. 41–end
Ps. 145 Song of Sol. 8. 5–7 John 11. 17–44 ct	**SATURDAY IN EASTER WEEK** Zech. 8. 1–8 Ps. 118. 14–21 1 Pet. 2. 1–10 W John 20. 24–end	Exod. 14. 15–end 1 Cor. 15. 51–end	Song of Sol. 8. 5–7 John 11. 17–44 ct

March 2008

			Sunday Principal Service / Weekday Eucharist	Third Service / Morning Prayer
30	S	**THE SECOND SUNDAY OF EASTER** *The reading from Acts must be used as either the first or second reading at the Principal Service.*	Acts 2. 14a, 22–32 [or Exod. 14. 10–end; 15. 20–21] Ps. 16 1 Pet. 1. 3–9 John 20. 19–end	Ps. 81. 1–10 Exod. 12. 1–17 1 Cor. 5. 6b–8
	W			
31	M ⓌⓌ	**THE ANNUNCIATION OF OUR LORD TO THE BLESSED VIRGIN MARY** (transferred from 25th)	Isa. 7. 10–14 Ps. 40. 5–11 Heb. 10. 4–10 Luke 1. 26–38	*MP*: Ps. 111; 113 1 Sam 2. 1–10 Rom. 5. 12–end

April 2008

1	Tu / W	**JOSEPH OF NAZARETH** (transferred from 19 March)	2 Sam. 7. 4–16 Ps. 89. 26–36 Rom. 4. 13–18 Matt. 1. 18–end	*MP*: Ps. 25; 147. 1–12 Isa. 11. 1–10 Matt. 13. 54–end
2	W / W		Acts 5. 17–26 Ps. 34. 1–8 John 3. 16–21	Ps. 16; **30** *alt.* Ps. 119. 1–32 Exod. 16. 11–end Col. 2. 1–15
3	Th / W		Acts 5. 27–33 Ps. 34. 1, 15–end John 3. 31–end	Ps. **28**; 29 *alt.* Ps. 14; **15**; 16 Exod. ch. 17 Col. 2.16 – 3.11
4	F / W		Acts 5. 34–42 Ps. 27. 1–5, 16–17 John 6. 1–15	Ps. 57; **61** *alt.* Ps. 17; **19** Exod. 18. 1–12 Col. 3.12 – 4.1
5	Sa / W		Acts 6. 1–7 Ps. 33. 1–5, 18–19 John 6. 16–21	Ps. 63; **84** *alt.* Ps. 20; 21; **23** Exod. 18. 13–end Col. 4. 2–end
6	S / W	**THE THIRD SUNDAY OF EASTER** *The reading from Acts must be used as either the first or second reading at the Principal Service.*	Acts 2. 14a, 36–41 [or Zeph. 3. 14–end] Ps. 116. 1–3, 10–end (or 116. 1–7) 1 Pet. 1. 17–23 Luke 24. 13–35	Ps. 23 Isa. 40. 1–11 1 Pet. 5. 1–11
7	M / W		Acts 6. 8–15 Ps. 119. 17–24 John 6. 22–29	Ps. **96**; 97 *alt.* Ps. 27; **30** Exod. ch. 19 Luke 1. 1–25
8	Tu / W		Acts 7.51 – 8.1 Ps. 31. 1–5, 16 John 6. 30–35	Ps. **98**; 99; 100 *alt.* Ps. **32**; 36 Exod. 20. 1–21 Luke 1. 26–38

Second Service Evening Prayer	Calendar and Holy Communion	Morning Prayer	Evening Prayer
	THE FIRST SUNDAY AFTER EASTER		
Ps. 30. 1–5 Dan. 6. [1–5] 6–23 Mark 15.46 – 16.8 or First EP of The Annunciation Ps. 85 Wisd. 9. 1–12 or Gen. 3. 8–15 Gal. 4. 1–5 ℣ ct	Ezek. 37. 1–10 Ps. 81. 1–4 1 John 5. 4–12 John 20. 19–23 W	Ps. 81. 1–10 Exod. 12. 1–17 1 Cor. 5. 6b–8	Ps. 30. 1–5 Dan. 6. [1–5] 6–23 Mark 15.46–16.8 or First EP of The Annunciation Ps. 85 Wisd. 9. 1–12 or Gen. 3. 8–15 Gal. 4. 1–5 ℣ ct
	THE ANNUNCIATION OF THE BLESSED VIRGIN MARY (transferred from 25th)		
EP: Ps. 131; 146 Isa. 52. 1–12 Heb. 2. 5–end	Isa. 7. 10–14 [15] Ps. 113 Rom. 5. 12–19 ℣ Luke 1. 26–38	Ps. 111 1 Sam 2. 1–10 Heb. 10. 4–10	Ps. 131; 146 Isa. 52. 1–12 Heb. 2. 5–end
EP: Ps. 1; 112 Gen. 50. 22–end Matt. 2. 13–end	To celebrate Joseph, see *Common Worship* provision Exod. 15.22 – 16.10 Col. 1. 15–end W		Deut. 1. 19–40 John 20. 11–18
Ps. 33 *alt.* Ps. **11**; 12; 13 Deut. 3. 18–end John 20. 19–end	W	Exod. 16. 11–end Col. 2. 1–15	Deut. 3. 18–end John 20. 19–end
Ps. 34 *alt.* Ps. 18† Deut. 4. 1–14 John 21. 1–14	**Richard, Bishop of Chichester, 1253** Com. Bishop W	Exod. ch. 17 Col. 2.16 – 3.11	Deut. 4. 1–14 John 21. 1–14
Ps. 118 *alt.* Ps. 22 Deut. 4. 15–31 John 21. 15–19	**Ambrose, Bishop of Milan, 397** Com. Doctor W	Exod. 18. 1–12 Col. 3.12 – 4.1	Deut. 4. 15–31 John 21. 15–19
Ps. 66 *alt.* Ps. **24**; 25 Deut. 4. 32–40 John 21. 20–end ct	W	Exod. 18. 13–end Col. 4. 2–end	Deut. 4. 32–40 John 21. 20–end ct
	THE SECOND SUNDAY AFTER EASTER		
Ps. 48 Hag. 1.13 – 2.9 1 Cor. 3. 10–17 *Gospel*: John 2. 13–22	Ezek. 34. 11–16a Ps. 23 1 Pet. 2. 19–end John 10. 11–16 W	Ps. 23 Isa. 40. 1–11 1 Pet. 5. 1–11	Ps. 48 Hag. 1.13 – 2.9 1 Cor. 3. 10–17
Ps. **61**; 65 *alt.* Ps. 26; **28**; 29 Deut. 5. 1–22 Eph. 1. 1–14	W	Exod. ch. 19 Luke 1. 1–25	Deut. 5. 1–22 Eph. 1. 1–14
Ps. 71 *alt.* Ps. 33 Deut. 5. 22–end Eph. 1. 15–end	W	Exod. 20. 1–21 Luke 1. 26–38	Deut. 5. 22–end Eph. 1. 15–end

April 2008

			Sunday Principal Service / Weekday Eucharist	Third Service / Morning Prayer
9	W	*Dietrich Bonhoeffer, Lutheran Pastor, Martyr, 1945*	Acts 8. 1b–8 Ps. 66. 1–6 John 6. 35–40	Ps. 105 *alt*. Ps. 34 Exod. ch. 24
	W			Luke 1. 39–56
10	Th	**William Law, Priest, Spiritual Writer, 1761** *William of Ockham, Friar, Philosopher, Teacher, 1347* Com. Teacher or *esp*. 1 Cor. 2. 9–end *also* Matt. 17. 1–9	Acts 8. 26–end Ps. 66. 7–8, 14–end John 6. 44–51	Ps. 136 *alt*. Ps. 37† Exod. 25. 1–22
	W			Luke 1. 57–end
11	F	*George Augustus Selwyn, first Bishop of New Zealand, 1878*	Acts 9. 1–20 Ps. 117 John 6. 52–59	Ps. 107 *alt*. Ps. 31 Exod. 28. 1–4a, 29–38
	W			Luke 2. 1–20
12	Sa		Acts 9. 31–42 Ps. 116. 10–15 John 6. 60–69	Ps. 108; *110*; 111 *alt*. Ps. 41; *42*; 43 Exod. 29. 1–9
	W			Luke 2. 21–40
13	S	**THE FOURTH SUNDAY OF EASTER** The reading from Acts must be used as either the first or second reading at the Principal Service.	Acts 2. 42–end [or Gen. ch. 7] Ps. 23 1 Pet. 2. 19–end John 10. 1–10	Ps. 106. 6–24 Neh. 9. 6–15 1 Cor. 10. 1–13
	W			
14	M		Acts 11. 1–18 Ps. 42. 1–2; 43. 1–4 John 10. 1–10 (*or* 11–18)	Ps. 103 *alt*. Ps. 44 Exod. 32. 1–14
	W			Luke 2. 41–end
15	Tu		Acts 11. 19–26 Ps. 87 John 10. 22–30	Ps. 139 *alt*. Ps. *48*; 52 Exod. 32. 15–34
	W			Luke 3. 1–14
16	W	*Isabella Gilmore, Deaconess, 1923*	Acts 12.24 – 13.5 Ps. 67 John 12. 44–end	Ps. 135 *alt*. Ps. 119. 57–80 Exod. ch. 33
	W			Luke 3. 15–22
17	Th		Acts 13. 13 – 25 Ps. 89. 1–2, 20–26 John 13. 16–20	Ps. 118 *alt*. Ps. 56; *57* (63†) Exod. 34. 1–10, 27–end
	W			Luke 4. 1–13
18	F		Acts 13. 26–33 Ps. 2 John 14. 1–6	Ps. 33 *alt*. Ps. *51*; 54 Exod. 35.20 – 36.7
	W			Luke 4. 14–30
19	Sa	**Alphege, Archbishop of Canterbury, Martyr, 1012** Com. Martyr or *also* Heb. 5. 1–4	Acts 13. 44–end Ps. 98. 1–5 John 14. 7–14	Ps. 34 *alt*. Ps. 68 Exod. 40. 17–end
	Wr			Luke 4. 31–37
20	S	**THE FIFTH SUNDAY OF EASTER** The reading from Acts must be used as either the first or second reading at the Principal Service.	Acts 7. 55–end [or Gen. 8. 1–19] Ps. 31. 1–5 [15–16] 1 Pet. 2. 2–10 John 14. 1–14	Ps. 30 Ezek. 37. 1–12 John 5. 19–29
	W			

BOOK OF COMMON PRAYER

Second Service Evening Prayer	Calendar and Holy Communion	Morning Prayer	Evening Prayer
Ps. 67; **72** alt. Ps. 119. 33–56 Deut. ch. 6 Eph. 2. 1–10	W	Exod. ch. 24 Luke 1. 39–56	Deut. ch. 6 Eph. 2. 1–10
Ps. 73 alt. Ps. 39; **40** Deut. 7. 1–11 Eph. 2. 11–end	W	Exod. 25. 1–22 Luke 1. 57–end	Deut. 7. 1–11 Eph. 2. 11–end
Ps. 77 alt. Ps. 35 Deut. 7. 12–end Eph. 3. 1–13	W	Exod. 28. 1–4a, 29–38 Luke 2. 1–20	Deut. 7. 12–end Eph. 3. 1–13
Ps. 23; **27** alt. Ps. 45; **46** Deut. ch. 8 Eph. 3. 14–end ct	W	Exod. 29. 1–9 Luke 2. 21–40	Deut. ch. 8 Eph. 3. 14–end ct
Ps. 29. 1–10 Ezra 3. 1–13 Eph. 2. 11–end *Gospel:* Luke 19. 37–end	**THE THIRD SUNDAY AFTER EASTER** Gen. 45. 3–10 Ps. 57 1 Pet. 2. 11–17 John 16. 16–22 W	Ps. 106. 6–24 Neh. 9. 6–15 1 Cor. 10. 1–13	Ps. 29. 1–10 Ezra 3. 1–13 Eph. 2. 11–end
Ps. 112; 113; **114** alt. Ps. **47**; 49 Deut. 9. 1–21 Eph. 4. 1–16	W	Exod. 32. 1–14 Luke 2. 41–end	Deut. 9. 1–21 Eph. 4. 1–16
Ps. 115; **116** alt. Ps. 50 Deut. 9.23 – 10.5 Eph. 4. 17–end	W	Exod. 32. 15–34 Luke 3. 1–14	Deut. 9.23 – 10.5 Eph. 4. 17–end
Ps. **47**; 48 alt. Ps. **59**; 60 (67) Deut. 10. 12–end Eph. 5. 1–14	W	Exod. ch. 33 Luke 3. 15–22	Deut. 10. 12–end Eph. 5. 1–14
Ps. 81; **85** alt. Ps. 61; **62**; 64 Deut. 11. 8–end Eph. 5. 15–end	W	Exod. 34. 1–10, 27–end Luke 4. 1–13	Deut. 11. 8–end Eph. 5. 15–end
Ps. **36**; 40 alt. Ps. 38 Deut. 12. 1–14 Eph. 6. 1–9	W	Exod. 35.20 – 36.7 Luke 4. 14–30	Deut. 12. 1–14 Eph. 6. 1–9
Ps. **84**; 86 alt. Ps. 65; **66** Deut. 15. 1–18 Eph. 6. 10–end ct	**Alphege, Archbishop of Canterbury, Martyr, 1012** Com. Martyr Wr	Exod. 40. 17–end Luke 4. 31–37	Deut. 15. 1–18 Eph. 6. 10–end ct
Ps. 147. 1–12 Zech. 4. 1–10 Rev. 21. 1–14 *Gospel:* Luke 2. 25–32 [33–38]	**THE FOURTH SUNDAY AFTER EASTER** Job 19. 21–27a Ps. 66. 14–end James 1. 17–21 John 16. 5–15 W	Ps. 30 Ezek. 37. 1–12 John 5. 19–29	Ps. 147. 1–12 Zech. 4. 1–10 Rev. 21. 1–14

April 2008

			Sunday Principal Service / Weekday Eucharist	Third Service / Morning Prayer
21	M W	**Anselm, Abbot of Le Bec, Archbishop of Canterbury, Teacher, 1109** Com. Teacher *also* Wisd. 9. 13–end Rom. 5. 8–11	*or* Acts 14. 5–18 Ps. 118. 1–3, 14–15 John 14. 21–26	Ps. 145 *alt.* Ps. 71 Num. 9. 15–end; 10. 33–end Luke 4. 38–end
22	Tu W		Acts 14. 19–end Ps. 145. 10–end John 14. 27–end	Ps. *19*; 147. 1–12 *alt.* Ps. 73 Num. 11. 1–33 Luke 5. 1–11
23	W R	**GEORGE, MARTYR, PATRON OF ENGLAND, c. 304**	1 Macc. 2. 59–64 *or* Rev. 12. 7–12 Ps. 126 2 Tim. 2. 3–13 John 15. 18–21	*MP:* Ps. 5; 146 Josh. 1. 1–9 Eph. 6. 10–20
24	Th W	*Mellitus, Bishop of London, first Bishop at St Paul's, 624*	Acts 15. 7–21 Ps. 96. 1–3, 7–10 John 15. 9–11	Ps. *57*; 148 *alt.* Ps. 78. 1–39† Num. 13. 1–3, 17–end Luke 5. 27–end
25	F R	**MARK THE EVANGELIST**	Prov. 15. 28–end *or* Acts 15. 35–end Ps. 119. 9–16 Eph. 4. 7–16 Mark 13. 5–13	*MP:* Ps. 37. 23–end; 148 Isa. 62. 6–10 *or* Ecclus. 51. 13–end Acts 12.25 – 13.13
26	Sa W		Acts 16. 1–10 Ps. 100 John 15. 18–21	Ps. *146*; 150 *alt.* Ps. *76*; 79 Num. 14. 26–end Luke 6. 12–26
27	S W	**THE SIXTH SUNDAY OF EASTER** *The reading from Acts must be used as either the first or second reading at the Principal Service*	Acts 17. 22–31 [*or* Gen. 8.20 – 9.17] Ps. 66. 7–18 1 Pet. 3. 13–end John 14. 15–21	Ps. 73. 21–28 Job 14. 1–2, 7–15; 19. 23–27a 1 Thess. 4. 13–end
28	M W	Rogation Day* *Peter Chanel, Missionary in the South Pacific, Martyr, 1841*	Acts 16. 11–15 Ps. 149. 1–5 John 15.26 – 16.4	Ps. *65*; 67 *alt.* Ps. *80*; 82 Num. 16. 1–35 Luke 6. 27–38
29	Tu W	**Catherine of Siena, Teacher, 1380** Rogation Day Com. Teacher *also* Prov. 8. 1, 6–11 John 17. 12–26	*or* Acts 16. 22–34 Ps. 138 John 16. 5–11	Ps. 124; 125; *126*; 127 *alt.* Ps. 87; *89. 1–18* Num. 16. 36–end Luke 6. 39–end
30	W W	Rogation Day* *Pandita Mary Ramabai, Translator of the Scriptures, 1922*	Acts 17.15, 22 – 18.1 Ps. 148. 1–2, 11–end John 16. 12–15	Ps. *132*; 133 *alt.* Ps. 119. 105–128 Num. 17. 1–11 Luke 7. 1–10

*For Rogation Day provision, see p. 12.

BOOK OF COMMON PRAYER

Second Service Evening Prayer	Calendar and Holy Communion	Morning Prayer	Evening Prayer
Ps. 105 alt. Ps. **72**; 75 Deut. 16. 1–20 1 Pet. 1. 1–12	W	Num. 9. 15–end; 10. 33–end Luke 4. 38–end	Deut. 16. 1–20 1 Pet. 1. 1–12
Ps. 96; **97** alt. Ps. 74 Deut. 17. 8–end 1 Pet. 1. 13–end or First EP of George: Ps. 111; 116 Jer. 15. 15–end Heb. 11.32 – 12.2 R ct	W	Num. 11. 1–33 Luke 5. 1–11	Deut. 17. 8–end 1 Pet. 1. 13–end or First EP of George: Ps. 111; 116 Jer. 15. 15–end Heb. 11.32 – 12.2 R ct
EP: Ps. 3; 11 Isa. 43. 1–7 John 15. 1–8	**George, Martyr, Patron of England, c. 304** To celebrate George, see *Common Worship* provision. Com. Martyr Wr	Num. ch. 12 Luke 5. 12–26	Deut. 18. 9–end 1 Pet. 2. 1–10
Ps. 104 alt. Ps. 78. 40–end† Deut. ch. 19 1 Pet. 2. 11–end or First EP of Mark: Ps. 19 Isa. 52. 7–10 Mark 1. 1–15 R ct	W	Num. 13. 1–3, 17–end Luke 5. 27–end	Deut. ch. 19 1 Pet. 2. 11–end or First EP of Mark (Ps. 19) Isa. 52. 7–10 Mark 1. 1–15 R ct
EP: Ps. 45 Ezek. 1. 4–14 2 Tim. 4. 1–11	**MARK THE EVANGELIST** Prov. 15. 28–end Ps. 119. 9–16 Eph. 4. 7–16 John 15. 1–11 R	(Ps. 37. 23–41; 148) Isa. 62. 6–10 or Ecclus. 51. 13–end Acts 12.25 – 13.13	(Ps. 45) Ezek. 1. 4–14 2 Tim. 4. 1–11
Ps. 118 alt. Ps. 81; **84** Deut. 24. 5–end 1 Pet. 3. 13–end ct	W	Num. 14. 26–end Luke 6. 12–26	Deut. 24. 5–end 1 Pet. 3. 13–end ct
Ps. 87; 36. 5–10 Zech. 8. 1–13 Rev. 21.22 – 22.5 Gospel: John 21. 1–14	**THE FIFTH SUNDAY AFTER EASTER** Rogation Sunday Joel 2. 21–26 Ps. 66. 1–8 James 1. 22–end John 16. 23b–end W	Ps. 73. 21–28 Job 14. 1–2, 7–15; 19. 23–27a 1 Thess. 4. 13–end	Ps. 87; 36. 5–10 Zech. 8. 1–13 Rev. 21.22 – 22.5
Ps. **121**; 122; 123 alt. Ps. **85**; 86 Deut. ch. 26 1 Pet. 4. 1–11	Rogation Day Job 28. 1–11 Ps. 107. 1–9 James 5. 7–11 Luke 6. 36–42 W	Num. 16. 1–35 Luke 6. 27–38	Deut. ch. 26 1 Pet. 4. 1–11
Ps. **128**; 129; 130; 131 alt. Ps. 89. 19–end Deut. 28. 1–14 1 Pet. 4. 12–end	Rogation Day Deut. 8. 1–10 Ps. 121 James 5. 16–end Luke 11. 5–13 W	Num. 16. 36–end Luke 6. 39–end	Deut. 28. 1–14 1 Pet. 4. 12–end
First EP of Ascension Day Ps. 15; 24 2 Sam. 23. 1–5 Col. 2.20 – 3.4 ℣ ct	Rogation Day Deut. 34. 1–7 Ps. 108. 1–6 Eph. 4. 7–13 John 17. 1–11 W	Num. 17. 1–11 Luke 7. 1–10	First EP of Ascension Day Ps. 15; 24 2 Sam. 23. 1–5 Col. 2.20 – 3.4 ℣ ct

May 2008

			Sunday Principal Service / Weekday Eucharist	Third Service / Morning Prayer
1	Th ⬧	**ASCENSION DAY** The reading from Acts must be used as either the first or second reading at the Eucharist.	Acts 1. 1–11 or Dan. 7. 9–14 Ps. 47 or Ps. 93 Eph. 1. 15–end or Acts 1. 1–11 Luke 24. 44–end	MP: Ps. 110; 150 Isa. 52. 7–end Heb. 7. [11–25] 26–end
2	F R	**PHILIP AND JAMES, APOSTLES** (transferred from 1 May)	Isa. 30. 15–21 Ps. 119. 1–8 Eph. 1. 3–10 John 14. 1–14	MP: Ps. 139; 146 Prov. 4. 10–18 James 1. 1–12
3	Sa W		Acts 18. 22–end Ps. 47. 1–2, 7–end John 16. 23–28	Ps. 21; **47** alt. Ps. 96; **97**; 100 Num. 21. 4–9 Luke 7. 18–35 [Num. 11. 16–17, 24–29 1 Cor. ch. 2]*
4	S W	**THE SEVENTH SUNDAY OF EASTER (SUNDAY AFTER ASCENSION DAY)** The reading from Acts must be used as either the first or second reading at the Principal Service	Acts 1. 6–14 [or Ezek. 36. 24–28] Ps. 68. 1–10 [32–35] 1 Pet. 4. 12–14; 5. 6–11 John 17. 1–11	Ps. 104. 26–35 Isa. 65. 17–end Rev. 21. 1–8
5	M W		Acts 19. 1–8 Ps. 68. 1–6 John 16. 29–end	Ps. **93**; 96; 97 alt. Ps. **98**; 99; 101 Num. 22. 1–35 Luke 7. 36–end [Num. 27. 15–end 1 Cor. ch. 3]
6	Tu W		Acts 20. 17–27 Ps. 68. 9–10, 18–19 John 17. 1–11	Ps. 98; **99**; 100 alt. Ps. **106**† (or 103) Num. 22.36 – 23.12 Luke 8. 1–15 [1 Sam. 10. 1–10 1 Cor. 12. 1–13]
7	W W		Acts 20. 28–end Ps. 68. 27–28, 32–end John 17. 11–19	Ps. 2; **29** alt. Ps. 110; **111**; 112 Num. 23. 13–end Luke 8. 16–25 [1 Kings 19. 1–18 Matt. 3. 13–end]
8	Th W	**Julian of Norwich, Spiritual Writer, c. 1417** Com. Religious also 1 Cor. 13. 8–end Matt. 5. 13–16	or Acts 22. 30; 23. 6–11 Ps. 16. 1, 5–end John 17. 20–end	Ps. **24**; 72 alt. Ps. 113; **115** Num. ch. 24 Luke 8. 26–39 [Ezek. 11. 14–20 Matt. 9.35 – 10.20]
9	F W		Acts 25. 13–21 Ps. 103. 1–2, 11–12, 19–20 John 21. 15–19	Ps. **28**; 30 alt. Ps. 139 Num. 27. 12–end Luke 8. 40–end [Ezek. 36. 22–28 Matt. 12. 22–32]

*The alternative readings in square brackets may be used at one of the offices, in preparation for the Day of Pentecost.

BOOK OF COMMON PRAYER

Second Service Evening Prayer	Calendar and Holy Communion	Morning Prayer	Evening Prayer
EP: Ps. 8 Song of the Three 29–37 or 2 Kings 2. 1–15 Rev. ch. 5 Gospel: Mark 16. 14–20	**ASCENSION DAY** Dan. 7. 13–14 Ps. 68. 1–6 Acts 1. 1–11 Mark 16. 14–20 or Luke 24. 44–end	Ps. 110; 150 Isa. 52. 7–end Heb. 7. [11–25] 26–end	Ps. 8 Song of the Three 29–37 or 2 Kings 2. 1–15 Rev. ch. 5
EP: Ps. 149 Job 23. 1–12 John 1. 43–end	**PHILIP AND JAMES, APOSTLES** Prov. 4. 10–18 Ps. 25. 1–9 James 1. [1]2–12 John 14. 1–14 R	(Ps. 139; 146) Isa. 30. 1–5 John 12. 20–26	(Ps. 149) Job 23. 1–12 John 1. 43–end
Ps. 84; **85** alt. Ps. 104 Deut. ch. 30 1 John 2. 7–17 ct	**The Invention of the Cross** Wr	Num. 21. 4–9 Luke 7. 18–35 [Num. 11. 16–17, 24–29 1 Cor. ch. 2]	Deut. ch. 30 1 John 2. 7–17 ct
Ps. 47 2 Sam. 23. 1–5 Eph. 1. 15–end Gospel: Mark 16. 14–20	**THE SUNDAY AFTER ASCENSION DAY** 2 Kings 2. 9–15 Ps. 68. 32–end 1 Pet. 4. 7–11 John 15.26 – 16.4a W	Ps. 104. 26–35 Isa. 65. 17–end Rev. 21. 1–8	Ps. 47 2 Sam. 23. 1–5 Eph. 1. 15–end
Ps. 18 alt. Ps. **105**† (or 103) Deut. 31. 1–13 1 John 2. 18–end	W	Num. 22. 1–35 Luke 7. 36–end [Num. 27. 15–end 1 Cor. ch. 3]	Deut. 31. 1–13 1 John 2. 18–end
Ps. 68 alt. Ps. 107† Deut. 31. 14–29 1 John 3. 1–10	**John the Evangelist, ante Portam Latinam** CEG of 27 December W	Num. 22.36 – 23.12 Luke 8. 1–15 [1 Sam. 10. 1–10 1 Cor. 12. 1–13]	Deut. 31. 14–29 1 John 3. 1–10
Ps. 36; **46** alt. Ps. 119. 129–152 Deut. 31.30 – 32.14 1 John 3. 11–end	W	Num. 23. 13–end Luke 8. 16–25 [1 Kings 19. 1–18 Matt. 3. 13–end]	Deut. 31.30 – 32.14 1 John 3. 11–end
Ps. 139 alt. Ps. 114; **116**; 117 Deut. 32. 15–47 1 John 4. 1–6	W	Num. ch. 24 Luke 8. 26–39 [Ezek. 11. 14–20 Matt. 9.35 – 10.20]	Deut. 32. 15–47 1 John 4. 1–6
Ps. 147 alt. Ps. **130**; 131; 137 Deut. ch. 33 1 John 4. 7–end	W	Num. 27. 12–end Luke 8. 40–end [Ezek. 36. 22–28 Matt. 12. 22–32]	Deut. ch. 33 1 John 4. 7–end

May 2008

			Sunday Principal Service / Weekday Eucharist	Third Service / Morning Prayer
10	Sa		Acts 28. 16–20, 30–end Ps. 11. 4–end John 21. 20–25	Ps. 42; **43** *alt.* Ps. 120; **121**; 122 Num. 32. 1–27 Luke 9. 1–17 [Mic. 3. 1–8 Eph. 6. 10–20]
	W			
11	S	**DAY OF PENTECOST (Whit Sunday)** The reading from Acts must be used as either the first or second reading at the Principal Service.	Acts 2. 1–21 or Num. 11. 24–30 Ps. 104. 26–34, 36, 37b (or 26–end) 1 Cor. 12. 3b–13 or Acts 2. 1–21 John 20. 19–23 or John 7. 37–39	MP: Ps. 87 Gen. 11. 1–9 Acts 10. 34–end
	R			
12 DEL 6	M	Ordinary Time resumes today	James 1. 1–11 Ps. 119. 65–72 Mark 8. 11–13	Ps. 123; 124; 125; **126** Josh. ch. 1 Luke 9. 18–27
	G			
13	Tu		James 1. 12–18 Ps. 94. 12–18 Mark 8. 14–21	Ps. **132**; 133 Josh. ch. 2 Luke 9. 28–36
	G			
14	W	**MATTHIAS THE APOSTLE*** The reading from Acts must be used as either the first or second reading at the Eucharist.	Isa. 22. 15–end or Acts 1. 15–end Ps. 15 Acts 1. 15–end or 1 Cor. 4. 1–7 John 15. 9–17	MP: Ps. 16; 147. 1–12 1 Sam. 2. 27–35 Acts 2. 37–end
	R			
	G	*or, if Matthias is celebrated on 25 February:*	James 1. 19–end Ps. 15 Mark 8. 22–26	Ps. 119. 153–end Josh. ch. 3 Luke 9. 37–50
15	Th		James 2. 1–9 Ps. 34. 1–7 Mark 8. 27–33	Ps. **143**; 146 Josh. 4.1 – 5.1 Luke 9. 51–end
	G			
16	F	Caroline Chisholm, Social Reformer, 1877	James 2. 14–24, 26 Ps. 112 Mark 8.34 – 9.1	Ps. **142**; 144 Josh. 5. 2–end Luke 10. 1–16
	G			
17	Sa		James 3. 1–10 Ps. 12. 1–7 Mark 9. 2–13	Ps. 147 Josh. 6. 1–20 Luke 10. 17–24
	G			

*Matthias may be celebrated on Monday 25 February instead of 14 May.

Second Service Evening Prayer	Calendar and Holy Communion	Morning Prayer	Evening Prayer
First EP of Pentecost Ps. 48 Deut. 16. 9–15 John 15.26 – 16.15 **R ct**	**W**	Num. 32. 1–27 Luke 9. 1–17 [Mic. 3. 1–8 Eph. 6. 10–20]	*First EP of Whit Sunday* Ps. 48 Deut. 16. 9–15 John 15.26 – 16.15 **R ct**
EP: Ps. 67; 133 Joel 2. 21–end Acts 2. 14–21 [22–38] *Gospel:* Luke 24. 44–end	**WHIT SUNDAY** Deut. 16. 9–12 Ps. 122 Acts 2. 1–11 John 14. 15–31a	Ps. 87 Gen. 11. 1–9 Acts 10. 34–end	Ps. 67; 133 Num. 11. 24–30 Acts 2. 14–21 [22–38]
	R		
Ps. *127*; 128; 129 Job ch. 1 Rom. 1. 1–17	**Monday in Whitsun Week** Acts 10. 34–end John 3. 16–21 **R**	Ezek. 11. 14–20 Acts 2. 12–36	Exod. 35.30 – 36.1 Acts 2. 37–end
Ps. (134); *135* Job ch. 2 Rom. 1. 18–end *or First EP of Matthias:* Ps. 147 Isa. 22. 15–22 Phil. 3.13b – 4.1 **R ct**	**Tuesday in Whitsun Week** Acts 8. 14–17 John 10. 1–10 **R**	Ezek. 37. 1–14 1 Cor. 12. 1–13	2 Sam. 23. 1–5 1 Cor. 12.27 – 13.end
EP: Ps. 80 1 Sam. 16. 1–13a Matt. 7. 15–27	Ember Day Ember CEG *or* Acts 2. 14–21 John 6. 44–51 **R**	Josh. ch. 3 Luke 9. 37–50	Job ch. 3 Rom. 2. 1–16
Ps. 136 Job ch. 3 Rom. 2. 1–16			
Ps. *138*; 140; 141 Job ch. 4 Rom. 2. 17–end	Acts 2. 22–28 Luke 9. 1–6 **R**	Josh. 4.1 – 5.1 Luke 9. 51–end	Job ch. 4 Rom. 2. 17–end
Ps. 145 Job ch. 5 Rom. 3. 1–20	Ember Day Ember CEG *or* Acts 8. 5–8 Luke 5. 17–26 **R**	Josh. 5. 2–end Luke 10. 1–16	Job ch. 5 Rom. 3. 1–20
First EP of Trinity Sunday Ps. 97; 98 Exod. 34. 1–10 Mark 1. 1–13 W ct	Ember Day Ember CEG *or* Acts 13. 44–end Matt. 20. 29–end **R**	Josh. 6. 1–20 Luke 10. 17–24	*First EP of Trinity Sunday* Ps. 97; 98 Exod. 34. 1–10 Mark 1. 1–13 W ct

May 2008

			Sunday Principal Service / Weekday Eucharist	Third Service / Morning Prayer
18	S	**TRINITY SUNDAY**	Isa. 40. 12–17, 27–end Ps. 8 2 Cor. 13. 11–end Matt. 28. 16–20	MP: Ps. 86. 8–13 Exod. 3. 1–6, 13–15 John 17. 1–11
	W			
19 DEL 7	M	**Dunstan, Archbishop of Canterbury, Restorer of Monastic Life, 988** Com. Bishop　　　　　　or *esp.* Matt. 24. 42–46 *also* Exod. 31. 1–5	James 3. 13–end Ps. 19. 7–end Mark 9. 14–29	Ps. *1*; 2; 3 Josh. 7. 1–15 Luke 10. 25–37
	Gw			
20	Tu	**Alcuin of York, Deacon, Abbot of Tours, 804** Com. Religious　　　　　or *also* Col. 3. 12–16 John 4. 19–24	James 4. 1–10 Ps. 55. 7–9, 24 Mark 9. 30–37	Ps. *5*; 6; (8) Josh. 7. 16–end Luke 10. 38–end
	Gw			
21	W	*Helena, Protector of the Holy Places, 330* 	James 4. 13–end Ps. 49. 1–2, 5–10 Mark 9. 38–40	Ps. 119. 1–32 Josh. 8. 1–29 Luke 11. 1–13
	G			
22	Th	**DAY OF THANKSGIVING FOR HOLY COMMUNION (CORPUS CHRISTI)**	Gen. 14. 18–20 Ps. 116. 10–end 1 Cor. 11. 23–26 John 6. 51–58	MP: Ps. 147 Deut. 8. 2–16 1 Cor. 10. 1–17
	W			
		or the ferial readings for the day:	James 5. 1–6 Ps. 49. 13–20 Mark 9. 41–50	Ps. 14; *15*; 16 Josh. 8. 30–end Luke 11. 14–28
	G			
23	F		James 5. 9–12 Ps. 103. 1–4, 8–13 Mark 10. 1–12	Ps. 17; *19* Josh. 9. 3–26 Luke 11. 29–36
	G			
24	Sa	**John and Charles Wesley, Evangelists, Hymn Writers, 1791 and 1788** Com. Pastor　　　　　　or *also* Eph. 5. 15–20	James 5. 13–end Ps. 141. 1–4 Mark 10. 13–16	Ps. 20; 21; *23* Josh. 10. 1–15 Luke 11. 37–end
	Gw			
25	S	**THE FIRST SUNDAY AFTER TRINITY (Proper 3)**	Lev. 19. 1–2, 9–18 Ps. 119. 33–40 1 Cor. 3. 10–11, 16–end Matt. 5. 38–end	Ps. 21; 23 Jer. 33. 1–11 Acts 8. 4–25
	G			
26 DEL 8	M	**Augustine, first Archbishop of Canterbury, 605** *John Calvin, Reformer, 1564; Philip Neri, Founder of the Oratorians, Spiritual Guide, 1595* Com. Bishop　　　　　　or *also* 1 Thess. 2. 2b–8 Matt. 13. 31–33	1 Pet. 1. 3–9 Ps. 111 Mark 10. 17–27	Ps. 27; *30* Josh. ch. 14 Luke 12. 1–12
	Gw			
27	Tu		1 Pet. 1. 10–16 Ps. 98. 1–5 Mark 10. 28–31	Ps. 32; *36* Josh. 21.43 – 22.8 Luke 12. 13–21
	G			
28	W	*Lanfranc, Prior of Le Bec, Archbishop of Canterbury, Scholar, 1089* 	1 Pet. 1. 18–end Ps. 147. 13–end Mark 10. 32–45	Ps. 34 Josh. 22. 9–end Luke 12. 22–31
	G			
29	Th		1 Pet. 2. 2–5, 9–12 Ps. 100 Mark 10. 46–end	Ps. 37† Josh. ch. 23 Luke 12. 32–40
	G			

BOOK OF COMMON PRAYER 49

Second Service Evening Prayer		Calendar and Holy Communion	Morning Prayer	Evening Prayer
		TRINITY SUNDAY		
EP: Ps. 93; 150		Isa. 6. 1–8	Ps. 86. 8–13	Ps. 93; 150
Isa. 6. 1–8		Ps. 8	Exod. 3. 1–6, 13–15	Isa. 40. 12–17, 27–end
John 16. 5–15		Rev. 4. 1–11	John 17. 1–11	John 16. 5–15
	⅏	John 3. 1–15		
		Dunstan, Archbishop of Canterbury, Restorer of Monastic Life, 988		
Ps. **4**; 7		Com. Bishop	Josh. 7. 1–15	Job ch. 7
Job ch. 7			Luke 10. 25–37	Rom. 4. 1–12
Rom. 4. 1–12	Gw			
Ps. **9**; 10†			Josh. 7. 16–end	Job ch. 8
Job ch. 8			Luke 10. 38–end	Rom. 4. 13–end
Rom. 4. 13–end	G			
Ps. *11*; 12; 13			Josh. 8. 1–29	Job ch. 9
Job ch. 9			Luke 11. 1–13	Rom. 5. 1–11
Rom. 5. 1–11				
or First EP of Corpus Christi				
Ps. 110; 111				
Exod. 16. 12–15				
John 6. 22–35				
W ct	G			
		To celebrate Corpus Christi, see *Common Worship* provision.		
EP: Ps. 23; 42; 43			Josh. 8. 30–end	Job ch. 10
Prov. 9. 1–5			Luke 11. 14–28	Rom. 5. 12–end
Luke 9. 11–17				
Ps. 18†				
Job ch. 10				
Rom. 5. 12–end	G			
Ps. 22			Josh. 9. 3–26	Job ch. 11
Job ch. 11			Luke 11. 29–36	Rom. 6. 1–14
Rom. 6. 1–14	G			
Ps. **24**; 25			Josh. 10. 1–15	Job ch. 12
Job ch. 12			Luke 11. 37–end	Rom. 6. 15–end
Rom. 6. 15–end				
ct	G			ct
		THE FIRST SUNDAY AFTER TRINITY		
Ps. 18. 1–20 (or 21–30)		2 Sam. 9. 6–end	Ps. 21; 23	Ps. 18. 1–20 (or 21–30)
Amos 9. 5–end		Ps. 41. 1–4	Jer. 33. 1–11	Amos 9. 5–end
Eph. 6. 1–20		1 John 4. 7–end	Acts 8. 4–25	Eph. 6. 1–20
Gospel: Mark 2. 1–12	G	Luke 16. 19–31		
		Augustine, first Archbishop of Canterbury, 605		
		Com. Bishop		
Ps. 26; **28**; 29			Josh. ch. 14	Job ch. 13
Job ch. 13			Luke 12. 1–12	Rom. 7. 1–6
Rom. 7. 1–6	Gw			
		The Venerable Bede, Monk at Jarrow, Scholar, Historian, 735		
Ps. 33		Com. Religious	Josh. 21.43 – 22.8	Job ch. 14
Job ch. 14			Luke 12. 13–21	Rom. 7. 7–end
Rom. 7. 7–end	Gw			
Ps. 119. 33–56			Josh. 22. 9–end	Job ch. 15
Job ch. 15			Luke 12. 22–31	Rom. 8. 1–11
Rom. 8. 1–11	G			
Ps. 39; **40**			Josh. ch. 23	Job 16.1 – 17.2
Job 16.1 – 17.2			Luke 12. 32–40	Rom. 8. 12–17
Rom. 8. 12–17	G			

May 2008

		Sunday Principal Service / Weekday Eucharist	Third Service Morning Prayer

30 F **Josephine Butler, Social Reformer, 1906**
Joan of Arc, Visionary, 1431; Apolo Kivebulaya, Priest, Evangelist in Central Africa, 1933

	Com. Saint	or	1 Pet. 4. 7–13	Ps. 31
	esp. Isa. 58. 6–11		Ps. 96. 10–end	Josh. 24. 1–28
	also 1 John 3. 18–23		Mark 11. 11–26	Luke 12. 41–48
	Matt. 9. 10–13			

Gw

31 Sa **THE VISIT OF THE BLESSED VIRGIN MARY TO ELIZABETH***

Zeph. 3. 14–18 MP: Ps. 85; 150
Ps. 113 1 Sam. 2. 1–10
Rom. 12. 9–16 Mark 3. 31–end
W Luke 1. 39–49 [50–56]

or, if The Visitation is celebrated on 2 July:

Jude 17, 20–end Ps. 41; **42**; 43
Ps. 63. 1–6 Josh. 24. 29–end
Mark 11. 27–end Luke 12. 49–end

June 2008

1 S **THE SECOND SUNDAY AFTER TRINITY (Proper 4)**
Track 1 Track 2 Ps. 37. 1–18
Gen. 6. 9–22; 7. 24; 8. 14–19 Deut. 11. 18–21, 26–28 Deut. 5. 1–21
Ps. 46 Ps. 31. [1–5] 19–24 Acts 21. 17–39a
Rom. 1. 16–17; 3. 22b–28 [29–31] Rom. 1. 16–17; 3. 22b–28
Matt. 7. 21–end [29–31]
G Matt. 7. 21–end

2 M   2 Pet. 1. 2–7 Ps. 44
DEL 9   Ps. 91. 1–2, 14–end Judg. ch. 2
G Mark 12. 1–12 Luke 13. 1–9

3 Tu *The Martyrs of Uganda, 1885–87 and 1977*
 2 Pet. 3. 11–15a, 17–end Ps. **48**; 52
 Ps. 90. 1–4, 10, 14, 16 Judg. 4. 1–23
G Mark 12. 13–17 Luke 13. 10–21

4 W *Petroc, Abbot of Padstow, 6th century*
 2 Tim. 1. 1–3, 6–12 Ps. 119. 57–80
 Ps. 123 Judg. ch. 5
G Mark 12. 18–27 Luke 13. 22–end

5 Th **Boniface (Wynfrith) of Crediton, Bishop, Apostle of Germany, Martyr, 754**
Com. Martyr or 2 Tim. 2. 8–15 Ps. 56; **57**; (63†)
also Acts 20. 24–28 Ps. 25. 4–12 Judg. 6. 1–24
Gr Mark 12. 28–34 Luke 14. 1–11

6 F *Ini Kopuria, Founder of the Melanesian Brotherhood, 1945*
 2 Tim. 3. 10–end Ps. **51**; 54
 Ps. 119. 161–168 Judg. 6. 25–end
G Mark 12. 35–37 Luke 14. 12–24

7 Sa   2 Tim. 4. 1–8 Ps. 68
   Ps. 71. 7–16 Judg. ch. 7
G Mark 12. 38–end Luke 14. 25–end

*The Visit of the Blessed Virgin Mary to Elizabeth may be celebrated on 2 July instead of 31 May.

Second Service Evening Prayer	Calendar and Holy Communion	Morning Prayer	Evening Prayer
Ps. 35 Job 17. 3–end Rom. 8. 18–30 or First EP of The Visit of Mary to Elizabeth Ps. 45 Song of Sol. 2. 8–14 Luke 1. 26–38 **W** ct	**G**	Josh. 24. 1–28 Luke 12. 41–48	Job 17. 3–end Rom. 8. 18–30
EP: Ps. 122; 127; 128 Zech. 2. 10–end John 3. 25–30	**G**	Josh. 24. 29–end Luke 12. 49–end	Job ch. 18 Rom. 8. 31–end ct
Ps. 45; **46** Job ch. 18 Rom. 8. 31–end ct			
	THE SECOND SUNDAY AFTER TRINITY		
Ps. 33. [1–11] 12–end Ruth 2. 1–20a Luke 8. 4–15	Gen. 12. 1–4 Ps. 120 1 John 3. 13–end Luke 14. 16–24 **G**	Ps. 37. 1–18 Deut. 5. 1–21 Acts 21. 17–39a	Ps. 33. [1–11] 12–end Ruth 2. 1–20a Luke 8. 4–15
Ps. **47**; 49 Job ch. 19 Rom. 9. 1–18	**G**	Judg. ch. 2 Luke 13. 1–9	Job ch. 19 Rom. 9. 1–18
Ps. 50 Job ch. 21 Rom. 9. 19–end	**G**	Judg. 4. 1–23 Luke 13. 10–21	Job ch. 21 Rom. 9. 19–end
Ps. **59**; 60; (67) Job ch. 22 Rom. 10. 1–10	**G**	Judg. ch. 5 Luke 13. 22–end	Job ch. 22 Rom. 10. 1–10
Ps. 61; **62**; 64 Job ch. 23 Rom. 10. 11–end	**Boniface (Wynfrith) of Crediton, Bishop, Apostle of Germany, Martyr, 754** Com. Martyr **Gr**	Judg. 6. 1–24 Luke 14. 1–11	Job ch. 23 Rom. 10. 11–end
Ps. 38 Job ch. 24 Rom. 11. 1–12	**G**	Judg. 6. 25–end Luke 14. 12–24	Job ch. 24 Rom. 11. 1–12
Ps. 65; **66** Job chs 25 – 26 Rom. 11. 13–24 ct	**G**	Judg. ch. 7 Luke 14. 25–end	Job chs 25 – 26 Rom. 11. 13–24 ct

June 2008

		Sunday Principal Service / Weekday Eucharist	Third Service / Morning Prayer

8 S — THE THIRD SUNDAY AFTER TRINITY (Proper 5)
Track 1
Gen. 12. 1–9
Ps. 33. 1–12
Rom. 4. 13–end
G   Matt. 9. 9–13, 18–26

Track 2
Hos. 5.15 – 6.6
Ps. 50. 7–15
Rom. 4. 13–25
Matt. 9. 9–13, 18–26

Ps. 38
Deut. 6. 10–end
Acts 22.22 – 23.11

9 M — **Columba, Abbot of Iona, Missionary, 597**
DEL 10   *Ephrem of Syria, Deacon, Hymn Writer, Teacher, 373*
Com. Missionary   *or*   1 Kings 17. 1–6
also Titus 2. 11–end   Ps. 121
Gw   Matt. 5. 1–12

Ps. 71
Judg. 8. 22–end
Luke 15. 1–10

10 Tu
1 Kings. 17. 7–16
Ps. 4
Matt. 5. 13–16

Ps. 73
Judg. 9. 1–21
Luke 15. 11–end

G

11 W — BARNABAS THE APOSTLE
The reading from Acts must be used as either the first or second reading at the Eucharist.
Job 29. 11–16
or Acts 11. 19–end
Ps. 112
Acts 11. 19–end
or Gal. 2. 1–10
R   John 15. 12–17

MP: Ps. 100; 101; 117
Jer. 9. 23–24
Acts 4. 32–end

12 Th
1 Kings 18. 41–end
Ps. 65. 8–end
G   Matt. 5. 20–26

Ps. 78. 1–39†
Judg. 11. 1–11
Luke 16. 19–end

13 F
1 Kings 19. 9, 11–16
Ps. 27. 8–16
G   Matt. 5. 27–32

Ps. 55
Judg. 11. 29–end
Luke 17. 1–10

14 Sa   *Richard Baxter, Puritan Divine, 1691*
1 Kings 19. 19–end
Ps. 16. 1–7
Matt. 5. 33–37
G

Ps. **76**; 79
Judg. 12. 1–7
Luke 17. 11–19

15 S — THE FOURTH SUNDAY AFTER TRINITY (Proper 6)
Track 1
Gen. 18. 1–15; [21. 1–7]
Ps. 116. 1, 10–17 (or 9–17)
Rom. 5. 1–8
G   Matt. 9.35 – 10.8 [9–23]

Track 2
Exod. 19. 2–8a
Ps. 100
Rom. 5. 1–8
Matt. 9.35 – 10.8 [9–23]

Ps. 45
Deut. 10.12 – 11.1
Acts 23. 12–end

16 M — **Richard, Bishop of Chichester, 1253**
DEL 11   *Joseph Butler, Bishop of Durham, Philosopher, 1752*
Com. Bishop   *or*   1 Kings 21. 1–16
also John 21. 15–19   Ps. 5. 1–5
Gw   Matt. 5. 38–42

Ps. **80**; 82
Judg. 13. 1–24
Luke 17. 20–end

17 Tu   *Samuel and Henrietta Barnett, Social Reformers, 1913 and 1936*
1 Kings 21. 17–end
Ps. 51. 1–9
G   Matt. 5. 43–end

Ps. 87; **89. 1–18**
Judg. ch. 14
Luke 18. 1–14

18 W   *Bernard Mizeki, Apostle of the MaShona, Martyr, 1896*
2 Kings 2. 1, 6–14
Ps. 31. 21–end
G   Matt. 6. 1–6, 16–18

Ps. 119. 105–128
Judg. 15.1 – 16.3
Luke 18. 15–30

Second Service Evening Prayer	Calendar and Holy Communion	Morning Prayer	Evening Prayer
	THE THIRD SUNDAY AFTER TRINITY		
Ps. [39]; 41 1 Sam. 18. 1–16 Luke 8. 41–end	2 Chron. 33. 9–13 Ps. 55. 17–23 1 Pet. 5. 5b–11 G Luke 15. 1–10	Ps. 38 Deut. 6. 10–end Acts 22.22 – 23.11	Ps. [39]; 41 1 Sam. 18. 1–16 Luke 8. 41–end
Ps. **72**; 75 Job ch. 27 Rom. 11. 25–end	G	Judg. 8. 22–end Luke 15. 1–10	Job ch. 27 Rom. 11. 25–end
Ps. 74 Job ch. 28 Rom. 12. 1–8 or First EP of Barnabas: Ps. 1; 15 Isa. 42. 5–12 Acts 14. 8–end **R ct**	G	Judg. 9. 1–21 Luke 15. 11–end	Job ch. 28 Rom. 12. 1–8 or First EP of Barnabas: (Ps. 1; 15) Isa. 42. 5–12 Acts 14. 8–end **R ct**
EP: Ps. 147 Eccles. 12. 9–end or Tobit 4. 5–11 Acts 9. 26–31	**BARNABAS THE APOSTLE** Job 29. 11–16 Ps. 112 Acts 11. 22–end John 15. 12–16 R	(Ps. 100; 101; 117) Jer. 9. 23–24 Acts 4. 32–end	(Ps. 147) Eccles. 12. 9–end or Tobit 4. 5–11 Acts 9. 26–31
Ps. 78. 40–end† Job ch. 30 Rom. 13. 1–7	G	Judg. 11. 1–11 Luke 16. 19–end	Job ch. 30 Rom. 13. 1–7
Ps. 69 Job ch. 31 Rom. 13. 8–end	G	Judg. 11. 29–end Luke 17. 1–10	Job ch. 31 Rom. 13. 8–end
Ps. 81; **84** Job ch. 32 Rom. 14. 1–12 ct	G	Judg. 12. 1–7 Luke 17. 11–19	Job ch. 32 Rom. 14. 1–12 ct
	THE FOURTH SUNDAY AFTER TRINITY		
Ps. [42]; 43 1 Sam. 21. 1–15 Luke 11. 14–28	Gen. 3. 17–19 Ps. 79. 8–10 Rom. 8. 18–23 G Luke 6. 36–42	Ps. 45 Deut. 10.12 – 11.1 Acts 23. 12–end	Ps. [42]; 43 1 Sam. 21. 1–15 Luke 11. 14–28
Ps. **85**; 86 Job ch. 33 Rom. 14. 13–end	G	Judg. 13. 1–24 Luke 17. 20–end	Job ch. 33 Rom. 14. 13–end
Ps. 89. 19–end Job ch. 38 Rom. 15. 1–13	**Alban, first Martyr of Britain, c. 250** Com. Martyr Gr	Judg. ch. 14 Luke 18. 1–14	Job ch. 38 Rom. 15. 1–13
Ps. **91**; 93 Job ch. 39 Rom. 15. 14–21	G	Judg. 15.1 – 16.3 Luke 18. 15–30	Job ch. 39 Rom. 15. 14–21

June 2008

			Sunday Principal Service / Weekday Eucharist	Third Service / Morning Prayer
19	Th	Sundar Singh of India, Sadhu (holy man), Evangelist, Teacher, 1929	Ecclus. 48. 1–14 or Isa. 63. 7–9 Ps. 97. 1–8 Matt. 6. 7–15	Ps. 90; **92** Judg. 16. 4–end Luke 18. 31–end
	G			
20	F		2 Kings 11. 1–4, 9–18, 20 Ps. 132. 1–5, 11–13 Matt. 6. 19–23	Ps. **88**; (95) Judg. ch. 17 Luke 19. 1–10
	G			
21	Sa		2 Chron. 24. 17–25 Ps. 89. 25–33 Matt. 6. 24–end	Ps. 96; **97**; 100 Judg. 18. 1–20, 27–end Luke 19. 11–27
	G			
22	S	**THE FIFTH SUNDAY AFTER TRINITY (Proper 7)** Track 1 Gen. 21. 8–21 Ps. 86. 1–10 [16–17] Rom. 6. 1b–11 Matt. 10. 24–39	Track 2 Jer. 20. 7–13 Ps. 69. 8–11 [12–17] 18–20 (or 14–20) Rom. 6. 1b–11 Matt. 10. 24–39	Ps. 49 Deut. 11. 1–15 Acts 27. 1–12
	G			
23 DEL 12	M	**Etheldreda, Abbess of Ely, c. 678** Com. Religious or also Matt. 25. 1–13	2 Kings 17. 5–8, 13–15, 18 Ps. 60. 1–5, 11–end Matt. 7. 1–5	Ps. **98**; 99; 101 1 Sam. 1. 1–20 Luke 19. 28–40
	Gw			
24	Tu	**THE BIRTH OF JOHN THE BAPTIST**	Isa. 40. 1–11 Ps. 85. 7–end Acts 13. 14b–26 or Gal. 3. 23–end Luke 1. 57–66, 80	MP: Ps. 50; 149 Ecclus. 48. 1–10 or Mal. 3. 1–6 Luke 3. 1–17
	W			
25	W	Ember Day*	2 Kings 22. 8–13; 23. 1–3 Ps. 119. 33–40 Matt. 7. 15–20	110; **111**; 112 1 Sam. 2. 12–26 Luke 20. 1–8
	G or R			
26	Th		2 Kings 24. 8–17 Ps. 79. 1–9, 12 Matt. 7. 21–end	Ps. 113; **115** 1 Sam. 2. 27–end Luke 20. 9–19
	G			
27	F	Ember Day* Cyril, Bishop of Alexandria, Teacher, 444	2 Kings 25. 1–12 Ps. 137. 1–6 Matt. 8. 1–4	Ps. 139 1 Sam. 3.1 – 4.1a Luke 20. 20–26
	G or R			
28	Sa	**Irenaeus, Bishop of Lyons, Teacher, c. 200** Ember Day* Com. Teacher or also 2 Pet. 1. 16–21	Lam. 2. 2, 10–14, 18–19 Ps. 74. 1–3, 21–end Matt. 8. 5–17	Ps. 120; **121**; 122 1 Sam. 4. 1b–end Luke 20. 27–40
	Gw or Rw			

*For Ember Day provision, see p. 13.

BOOK OF COMMON PRAYER 55

Second Service Evening Prayer		Calendar and Holy Communion	Morning Prayer	Evening Prayer
Ps. 94 Job ch. 40 Rom. 15. 22–end	G		Judg. 16. 4–end Luke 18. 31–end	Job ch. 40 Rom. 15. 22–end
Ps. 102 Job ch. 41 Rom. 16. 1–16	Gr	**Translation of Edward, King of the West Saxons, 979** Com. Martyr	Judg. ch. 17 Luke 19. 1–10	Job ch. 41 Rom. 16. 1–16
Ps. 104 Job ch. 42 Rom. 16. 17–end ct	G		Judg. 18. 1–20, 27–end Luke 19. 11–27	Job ch. 42 Rom. 16. 17–end ct
Ps. 46; [48] 1 Sam. 24. 1–17 Luke 14. 12–24	G	**THE FIFTH SUNDAY AFTER TRINITY** 1 Kings 19. 19–21 Ps. 84. 8–end 1 Pet. 3. 8–15a Luke 5. 1–11	Ps. 49 Deut. 11. 1–15 Acts 27. 1–12	Ps. 46; [48] 1 Sam. 24. 1–17 Luke 14. 1–14
Ps. 105† (or 103) Ezek. 1. 1–14 2 Cor. 1. 1–14 or First EP of The Birth of John the Baptist Ps. 71 Judg. 13. 2–7, 24–end Luke 1. 5–25 W ct	G		1 Sam. 1. 1–20 Luke 19. 28–40	Ezek. 1. 1–14 2 Cor. 1. 1–14 or First EP of The Nativity of John the Baptist (Ps. 71) Judg. 13. 2–7, 24–end Luke 1. 5–25 W ct
EP: Ps. 80; 82 Mal. ch. 4 Matt. 11. 2–19	W	**THE NATIVITY OF JOHN THE BAPTIST** Isa. 40. 1–11 Ps. 80. 1–7 Acts 13. 22–26 Luke 1. 57–80	(Ps. 50; 149) Ecclus. 48. 1–10 or Mal. 3. 1–6 Luke 3. 1–17	(Ps. 82) Mal. ch. 4 Matt. 11. 2–19
Ps. 119. 129–152 Ezek. 2.3 – 3.11 2 Cor. 2. 5–end	G		1 Sam. 2. 12–26 Luke 20. 1–8	Ezek. 2.3 – 3.11 2 Cor. 2. 5–end
Ps. 114; 116; 117 Ezek. 3. 12–end 2 Cor. ch. 3	G		1 Sam. 2. 27–end Luke 20. 9–19	Ezek. 3. 12–end 2 Cor. ch. 3
Ps. 130; 131; 137 Ezek. ch. 8 2 Cor. ch. 4	G		1 Sam. 3.1 – 4.1a Luke 20. 20–26	Ezek. ch. 8 2 Cor. ch. 4
Ps. 118 Ezek. ch. 9 2 Cor. ch. 5 ct or First EP of Peter and Paul Ps. 66; 67 Ezek. 3. 4–11 Gal. 1.13 – 2.8 or, for Peter alone: Acts 9. 32–end R ct	G		1 Sam. 4. 1b–end Luke 20. 27–40	Ezek. ch. 9 2 Cor. ch. 5 ct or First EP of Peter (Ps. 66; 67) Ezek. 3. 4–11 Acts 9. 32–end R ct

June 2008

			Sunday Principal Service / Weekday Eucharist	Third Service / Morning Prayer
29	S	**PETER AND PAUL, APOSTLES** (or transferred to 30th) The reading from Acts must be used as either the first or second reading at the Eucharist.	Zech. 4. 1–6a, 10b–end or Acts 12. 1–11 Ps. 125 Acts 12. 1–11 or 2 Tim. 4. 6–8, 17–18	MP: Ps. 71; 113 Isa. 49. 1–6 Acts 11. 1–18
	R		Matt. 16. 13–19	
		or, if Peter is commemorated alone: The reading from Acts must be used as either the first or second reading at the Eucharist.	Ezek. 3. 22–end or Acts 12. 1–11 Ps. 125 Acts 12. 1–11 or 1 Pet. 2. 19–end	MP: Ps. 71; 113 Isa. 49. 1–6 Acts 11. 1–18
	R		Matt. 16. 13–19	
		or, for The Sixth Sunday after Trinity (Proper 8) Track 1 Gen. 22. 1–14 Ps. 13 Rom. 6. 12–end	Track 2 Jer. 28. 5–9 Ps. 89. 1–4, 15–18 (or 8–18) Rom. 6. 12–23	Ps. 52; 53 Deut. 15. 1–11 Acts 27. [13–32] 33–end
	G		Matt. 10. 40–end	Matt. 10. 40–42
30 DEL 13	M	For Peter and Paul, see 29th	Amos 2. 6–10, 13–end Ps. 50. 16–23	Ps. 123; 124; 125; **126** 1 Sam. ch. 5
	G		Matt. 8. 18–22	Luke 20.41 – 21.4

July 2008

1	Tu	Henry, John and Henry Venn the Younger, Priests, Evangelical Divines, 1797, 1813 and 1873	Amos 3. 1–8; 4. 11–12 Ps. 5. 8–end	Ps. **132**; 133 1 Sam. 6. 1–16
	G		Matt. 8. 23–27	Luke 21. 5–19
2	W		Amos 5. 14–15, 21–24 Ps. 50. 7–14 Matt. 8. 28–end	Ps. 119. 153–end 1 Sam. ch. 7 Luke 21. 20–28
	G			
3	Th	**THOMAS THE APOSTLE***	Hab. 2. 1–4 Ps. 31. 1–6 Eph. 2. 19–end	MP: Ps. 92; 146 2 Sam. 15. 17–21 or Ecclus. ch. 2
	R		John 20. 24–29	John 11. 1–16
		or, if Thomas is not celebrated:	Amos 7. 10–end Ps. 19. 7–10	Ps. **143**; 146 1 Sam. ch. 8
	G		Matt. 9. 1–8	Luke 21. 29–end
4	F		Amos 8. 4–6, 9–12 Ps. 119. 1–8	Ps. 142; **144** 1 Sam. 9. 1–14
	G		Matt. 9. 9–13	Luke 22. 1–13
5	Sa		Amos 9. 11–end Ps. 85. 8–end	Ps. 147 1 Sam. 9.15 – 10.1
	G		Matt. 9. 14–17	Luke 22. 14–23

*Thomas the Apostle may be celebrated on Monday 22 December instead of 3 July.

BOOK OF COMMON PRAYER

Second Service Evening Prayer		Calendar and Holy Communion	Morning Prayer	Evening Prayer
EP: Ps. 124; 138 Ezek. 34. 11–16 John 21. 15–22	R	**PETER THE APOSTLE** (or transferred to 30th) Ezek. 3. 4–11 Ps. 125 Acts 12. 1–11 Matt. 16. 13–19	(Ps. 71; 113) Isa. 49. 1–6 Acts 11. 1–18	(Ps. 124; 138) Ezek. 34. 11–16 John 21. 15–22
EP: Ps. 124; 138 Ezek. 34. 11–16 John 21. 15–22				
Ps. 50. 1–15 [16–end] 1 Sam. 28. 3–19 Luke 17. 20–end	G	or, for The Sixth Sunday after Trinity Gen. 4. 2b–15 Ps. 90. 12–end Rom. 6. 3–11 Matt. 5. 20–26	Ps. 52; 53 Deut. 15. 1–11 Acts 27. [13–32] 33–end	Ps. 50. 1–15 [16–end] 1 Sam. 28. 3–19 Luke 17. 20–end
Ps. *127*; 128; 129 Ezek. 10. 1–19 2 Cor. 6.1 – 7.1	G	For Peter, see 29th	1 Sam. ch. 5 Luke 20.41 – 21.4	Ezek. 10. 1–19 2 Cor. 6.1 – 7.1
Ps. (134); *135* Ezek. 11. 14–end 2 Cor. 7. 2–end	G		1 Sam. 6. 1–16 Luke 21. 5–19	Ezek. 11. 14–end 2 Cor. 7. 2–end
Ps. 136 Ezek. 12. 1–16 2 Cor. 8. 1–15 or First EP of Thomas Ps. 27 Isa. ch. 35 Heb. 10.35 – 11.1 **R** ct	Gw	**The Visitation of the Blessed Virgin Mary*** 1 Sam. 2. 1–3 Ps. 113 Gal. 4. 1–5 Luke 1. 39–45	1 Sam. ch. 7 Luke 21. 20–28	Ezek. 12. 1–16 2 Cor. 8. 1–15
EP: Ps. 139 Job 42. 1–6 1 Pet. 1. 3–12	G		1 Sam. ch. 8 Luke 21. 29–end	Ezek. 12. 17–end 2 Cor. 8.16 – 9.5
Ps. *138*; 140; 141 Ezek. 12. 17–end 2 Cor. 8.16 – 9.5				
Ps. 145 Ezek. 13. 1–16 2 Cor. 9. 6–end	Gw	**Translation of Martin, Bishop of Tours, c. 397** Com. Bishop	1 Sam. 9. 1–14 Luke 22. 1–13	Ezek. 13. 1–16 2 Cor. 9. 6–end
Ps. *148*; 149; 150 Ezek. 14. 1–11 2 Cor. ch. 10 ct	G		1 Sam. 9.15 – 10.1 Luke 22. 14–23	Ezek. 14. 1–11 2 Cor. ch. 10 ct

*Common Worship Morning and Evening Prayer provision for 31 May may be used.

July 2008

		Sunday Principal Service / Weekday Eucharist	Third Service / Morning Prayer

6 S — THE SEVENTH SUNDAY AFTER TRINITY (Proper 9)
  Track 1
  Gen. 24. 34–38, 42–49, 58–end
  Ps. 45. 10–17
  or Canticle: Song of Sol. 2. 8–13
  Rom. 7. 15–25a
  G Matt. 11. 16–19, 25–end

  Track 2
  Zech. 9. 9–12
  Ps. 145. 8–15
  Rom. 7. 15–25a
  Matt. 11. 16–19, 25–30

  Ps. 55. 1–15, 18–22
  Deut. 24. 10–end
  Acts 28. 1–16

7 M*
DEL 14 G
  Hos. 2. 16–18, 21–22
  Ps. 145. 2–9
  Matt. 9. 18–26

  Ps. 1; 2; 3
  1 Sam. 10. 1–16
  Luke 22. 24–30

8 Tu
  G
  Hos. 8. 4–7, 11–13
  Ps. 103. 8–12
  Matt. 9. 32–end

  Ps. 5; 6; (8)
  1 Sam. 10. 17–end
  Luke 22. 31–38

9 W
  G
  Hos. 10. 1–3, 7–8, 12
  Ps. 115. 3–10
  Matt. 10. 1–7

  Ps. 119. 1–32
  1 Sam. ch. 11
  Luke 22. 39–46

10 Th
  G
  Hos. 11. 1, 3–4, 8–9
  Ps. 105. 1–7
  Matt. 10. 7–15

  Ps. 14; *15*; 16
  1 Sam. ch. 12
  Luke 22. 47–62

11 F — Benedict of Nursia, Abbot of Monte Cassino, Father of Western Monasticism, c. 550
  Com. Religious   or   Hos. 14. 2–end
  also 1 Cor. 3. 10–11   Ps. 80. 1–7
  Gw Luke 18. 18–22   Matt. 10. 16–23

  Ps. 17; *19*
  1 Sam. 13. 5–18
  Luke 22. 63–end

12 Sa
  G
  Isa. 6. 1–8
  Ps. 51. 1–7
  Matt. 10. 24–33

  Ps. 20; 21; *23*
  1 Sam. 13.19 – 14.15
  Luke 23. 1–12

13 S — THE EIGHTH SUNDAY AFTER TRINITY (Proper 10)
  Track 1
  Gen. 25. 19–end
  Ps. 119. 105–112
  Rom. 8. 1–11
  G Matt. 13. 1–9, 18–23

  Track 2
  Isa. 55. 10–13
  Ps. 65. [1–7] 8–end
  Rom. 8. 1–11
  Matt. 13. 1–9, 18–23

  Ps. 64; 65
  Deut. 28. 1–14
  Acts 28. 17–end

14 M — John Keble, Priest, Tractarian, Poet, 1866
DEL 15   Com. Pastor   or   Isa. 1. 11–17
  also Lam. 3. 19–26   Ps. 50. 7–15
  Gw Matt. 5. 1–8   Matt. 10.34 – 11.1

  Ps. 27; *30*
  1 Sam. 14. 24–46
  Luke 23. 13–25

15 Tu — Swithun, Bishop of Winchester, c. 862
  Bonaventure, Friar, Bishop, Teacher, 1274
  Com. Bishop   or   Isa. 7. 1–9
  also James 5. 7–11, 13–18   Ps. 48. 1–7
  Gw   Matt. 11. 20–24

  Ps. 32; *36*
  1 Sam. 15. 1–23
  Luke 23. 26–43

16 W — Osmund, Bishop of Salisbury, 1099
  G
  Isa. 10. 5–7, 13–16
  Ps. 94. 5–11
  Matt. 11. 25–27

  Ps. 34
  1 Sam. ch. 16
  Luke 23. 44–56a

17 Th
  G
  Isa. 26. 7–9, 16–19
  Ps. 102. 14–21
  Matt. 11. 28–end

  Ps. 37†
  1 Sam. 17. 1–30
  Luke 23.56b – 24.12

18 F — Elizabeth Ferard, first deaconess of the Church of England, Founder of the Community of St Andrew, 1883
  Isa. 38. 1–6, 21–22, 7–8
  Canticle: Isa. 38. 10–16
  or Ps. 32. 1–8
  G Matt. 12. 1–8

  Ps. 31
  1 Sam. 17. 31–54
  Luke 24. 13–35

*Thomas Becket may be celebrated on 7 July instead of 29 December.

BOOK OF COMMON PRAYER

Second Service Evening Prayer	Calendar and Holy Communion	Morning Prayer	Evening Prayer
	THE SEVENTH SUNDAY AFTER TRINITY		
Ps. 56; [57] 2 Sam. 2. 1–11; 3. 1 Luke 18.31 – 19.10	1 Kings 17. 8–16 Ps. 34. 11–end Rom. 6. 19–end Mark 8. 1–10a G	Ps. 55. 1–15, 18–22 Deut. 24. 10–end Acts 28. 1–16	Ps. 56; [57] 2 Sam. 2. 1–11; 3. 1 Luke 18.31 – 19.10
Ps. *4*; 7 Ezek. 14. 12–end 2 Cor. 11. 1–15	G	1 Sam. 10. 1–16 Luke 22. 24–30	Ezek. 14. 12–end 2 Cor. 11. 1–15
Ps. *9*; 10† Ezek. 18. 1–20 2 Cor. 11. 16–end	G	1 Sam. 10. 17–end Luke 22. 31–38	Ezek. 18. 1–20 2 Cor. 11. 16–end
Ps. *11*; 12; 13 Ezek. 18. 21–32 2 Cor. ch. 12	G	1 Sam. ch. 11 Luke 22. 39–46	Ezek. 18. 21–32 2 Cor. ch. 12
Ps. 18† Ezek. 20. 1–20 2 Cor. ch. 13	G	1 Sam. ch. 12 Luke 22. 47–62	Ezek. 20. 1–20 2 Cor. ch. 13
Ps. 22 Ezek. 20. 21–38 James 1. 1–11	G	1 Sam. 13. 5–18 Luke 22. 63–end	Ezek. 20. 21–38 James 1. 1–11
Ps. *24*; 25 Ezek. 24. 15–end James 1. 12–end ct	G	1 Sam. 13.19 – 14.15 Luke 23. 1–12	Ezek. 24. 15–end James 1. 12–end ct
	THE EIGHTH SUNDAY AFTER TRINITY		
Ps. 60; [63] 2 Sam. 7. 18–end Luke 19.41 – 20.8	Jer. 23. 16–24 Ps. 31. 1–6 Rom. 8. 12–17 Matt. 7. 15–21 G	Ps. 64; 65 Deut. 28. 1–14 Acts 28. 17–end	Ps. 60; [63] 2 Sam. 7. 18–end Luke 20. 1–8
Ps. 26; *28*; 29 Ezek. 28. 1–19 James 2. 1–13	G	1 Sam. 14. 24–46 Luke 23. 13–25	Ezek. 28. 1–19 James 2. 1–13
Ps. 33 Ezek. 33. 1–20 James 2. 14–end	**Swithun, Bishop of Winchester, c. 862** Com. Bishop Gw	1 Sam. 15. 1–23 Luke 23. 26–43	Ezek. 33. 1–20 James 2. 14–end
Ps. 119. 33–56 Ezek. 33. 21–end James ch. 3	G	1 Sam. ch. 16 Luke 23. 44–56a	Ezek. 33. 21–end James ch. 3
Ps. 39; *40* Ezek. 34. 1–16 James 4. 1–12	G	1 Sam. 17. 1–30 Luke 23.56b – 24.12	Ezek. 34. 1–16 James 4. 1–12
Ps. 35 Ezek. 34. 17–end James 4.13 – 5.6	G	1 Sam. 17. 31–54 Luke 24. 13–35	Ezek. 34. 17–end James 4.13 – 5.6

July 2008

			Sunday Principal Service / Weekday Eucharist	Third Service / Morning Prayer

19 Sa — **Gregory, Bishop of Nyssa, and his sister Macrina, Deaconess, Teachers, c. 394 and c. 379**
Com. Teacher *or* Mic. 2. 1–5
esp. 1 Cor. 2. 9–13
also Wisd. 9. 13–17
Ps. 10. 1–5a, 12
Matt. 12. 14–21
Ps. 41; **42**; 43
1 Sam. 17.55 – 18.16
Luke 24. 36–end
Gw

20 S — **THE NINTH SUNDAY AFTER TRINITY (Proper 11)**
Track 1
Gen. 28. 10–19a
Ps. 139. 1–11 [23–24]
Rom. 8. 12–25
Matt. 13. 24–30, 36–43

Track 2
Wisd. 12. 13, 16–19
or Isa. 44. 6–8
Ps. 86. 11–17
Rom. 8. 12–25
Matt. 13. 24–30, 36–43

Ps. 71
Deut. 30. 1–10
1 Pet. 3. 8–18
G

21 M
DEL 16
Mic. 6. 1–4, 6–8
Ps. 50. 3–7, 14
Matt. 12. 38–42
Ps. 44
1 Sam. 19. 1–18
Acts 1. 1–14

G

22 Tu — **MARY MAGDALENE**
Song of Sol. 3. 1–4
Ps. 42. 1–10
2 Cor. 5. 14–17
John 20. 1–2, 11–18
MP: Ps. 30; 32; 150
1 Sam. 16. 14–end
Luke 8. 1–3
W

23 W — *Bridget of Sweden, Abbess of Vadstena, 1373*
Jer. 1. 1, 4–10
Ps. 70
Matt. 13. 1–9
Ps. 119. 57–80
1 Sam. 20. 18–end
Acts 2. 1–21
G

24 Th
Jer. 2. 1–3, 7–8, 12–13
Ps. 36. 5–10
Matt. 13. 10–17
Ps. 56; **57**; (63†)
1 Sam. 21.1 – 22.5
Acts 2. 22–36

G

25 F — **JAMES THE APOSTLE**
The reading from Acts must be used as either the first or second reading at the Principal Service.
Jer. 45. 1–5
or Acts 11.27 – 12.2
Ps. 126
Acts 11.27 – 12.2
or 2 Cor. 4. 7–15
Matt. 20. 20–28
MP: Ps. 7; 29; 117
2 Kings 1. 9–15
Luke 9. 46–56
R

26 Sa — **Anne and Joachim, Parents of the Blessed Virgin Mary**
Zeph. 3. 14–18a *or* Jer. 7. 1–11
Ps. 127
Rom. 8. 28–30
Matt. 13. 16–17
Ps. 84. 1–6
Matt. 13. 24–30
Ps. 68
1 Sam. ch. 23
Acts 3. 1–10
Gw

27 S — **THE TENTH SUNDAY AFTER TRINITY (Proper 12)**
Track 1
Gen. 29. 15–28
Ps. 105. 1–11 [45b]
or Ps. 128
Rom. 8. 26–end
Matt. 13. 31–33, 44–52

Track 2
1 Kings 3. 5–12
Ps. 119. 129–136
Rom. 8. 26–39
Matt. 13. 31–33, 44–52

Ps. 77
Song of Sol. ch. 2
or 1 Macc. 2. [1–14] 15–22
1 Pet. 4. 7–14
G

BOOK OF COMMON PRAYER 61

Second Service Evening Prayer	Calendar and Holy Communion	Morning Prayer	Evening Prayer
Ps. 45; **46** Ezek. 36. 16–36 James 5. 7–end **ct**	**G**	1 Sam. 17.55 – 18.16 Luke 24. 36–end	Ezek. 36. 16–36 James 5. 7–end **ct**
Ps. 67; [70] 1 Kings 2. 10–12; 3. 16–end Acts 4. 1–22 Gospel: Mark 6. 30–34, 53–end	**THE NINTH SUNDAY AFTER TRINITY** Num. 10.35 – 11.3 Ps. 95 1 Cor. 10. 1–13 Luke 16. 1–9 or Luke 15. 11–end **G**	Ps. 71 Deut. 30. 1–10 1 Pet. 3. 13–22	Ps. 67; [70] 1 Kings 2. 10–12; 3. 16–end Acts 4. 1–22
Ps. **47**; 49 Ezek. 37. 1–14 Mark 1. 1–13 or First EP of Mary Magdalene Ps. 139 Isa. 25. 1–9 2 Cor. 1. 3–7 **W ct**	**G**	1 Sam. 19. 1–18 Acts 1. 1–14	Ezek. 37. 1–14 Mark 1. 1–13 or First EP of Mary Magdalene (Ps. 139) Isa. 25. 1–9 2 Cor. 1. 3–7 **W ct**
EP: Ps. 63 Zeph. 3. 14–end Mark 15.40 – 16.7	**MARY MAGDALENE** Zeph. 3. 14–end Ps. 30. 1–5 2 Cor. 5. 14–17 John 20. 11–18 **W**	(Ps. 30; 32; 150) 1 Sam. 16. 14–end Luke 8. 1–3	(Ps. 63) Song of Sol. 3. 1–4 Mark 15.40 – 16.7
Ps. **59**; 60 (67) Ezek. 39. 21–end Mark 1. 21–28	**G**	1 Sam. 20. 18–end Acts 2. 1–21	Ezek. 39. 21–end Mark 1. 21–28
Ps. 61; **62**; 64 Ezek. 43. 1–12 Mark 1. 29–end or First EP of James Ps. 144 Deut. 30. 11–end Mark 5. 21–end **R ct**	**G**	1 Sam. 21.1 – 22.5 Acts 2. 22–36	Ezek. 43. 1–12 Mark 1. 29–end or First EP of James (Ps. 144) Deut. 30. 11–end Mark 5. 21–end **R ct**
EP: Ps. 94 Jer. 26. 1–15 Mark 1. 14–20	**JAMES THE APOSTLE** 2 Kings 1. 9–15 Ps. 15 Acts 11.27 – 12.3a Matt. 20. 20–28 **R**	(Ps. 7; 29; 117) Jer. 45. 1–5 Luke 9. 46–56	(Ps. 94) Jer. 26. 1–15 Mark 1. 14–20
Ps. 65; **66** Ezek. 47. 1–12 Mark 2. 13–22 **ct**	**Anne, Mother of the Blessed Virgin Mary** Com. Saint **Gw**	1 Sam. ch. 23 Acts 3. 1–10	Ezek. 47. 1–12 Mark 2. 13–22 **ct**
Ps. 75; [76] 1 Kings 6. 11–14, 23–end Acts 12. 1–17 Gospel: John 6. 1–21	**THE TENTH SUNDAY AFTER TRINITY** Jer. 7. 9–15 Ps. 17. 1–8 1 Cor. 12. 1–11 Luke 19. 41–47a **G**	Ps. 77 Song of Sol. ch. 2 or 1 Macc. 2. [1–14] 15–22 1 Pet. 4. 7–14	Ps. 75; [76] 1 Kings 6. 11–14, 23–end Acts 12. 1–17

July 2008

		Sunday Principal Service / Weekday Eucharist	Third Service / Morning Prayer
28 DEL 17	M G	Jer. 13. 1–11 Ps. 82 or Deut. 32. 18–21 Matt. 13. 31–35	Ps. 71 1 Sam. ch. 24 Acts 3. 11–end
29	Tu Gw	**Mary, Martha and Lazarus, Companions of Our Lord** Isa. 25. 6–9 or Jer. 14. 17–end Ps. 49. 1–10, 16 Ps. 79. 8–end Heb. 2. 10–15 Matt. 13. 36–43 John 12. 1–8	Ps. 73 1 Sam. ch. 26 Acts 4. 1–12
30	W Gw	**William Wilberforce, Social Reformer, 1833** Com. Saint or Jer. 15. 10, 16–end also Job 31. 16–23 Ps. 59. 1–4, 18–end Gal. 3. 26–end; 4. 6–7 Matt. 13. 44–46 Luke 4. 16–21	Ps. 77 1 Sam. 28. 3–end Acts 4. 13–31
31	Th G	*Ignatius of Loyola, Founder of the Society of Jesus, 1556* Jer. 18. 1–6 Ps. 146. 1–5 Matt. 13. 47–53	Ps. 78. 1–39† 1 Sam. ch. 31 Acts 4.32 – 5.11

August 2008

1	F G	Jer. 26. 1–9 Ps. 69. 4–10 Matt. 13. 54–end	Ps. 55 2 Sam. ch. 1 Acts 5. 12–26
2	Sa G	Jer. 26. 11–16, 24 Ps. 69. 14–20 Matt. 14. 1–12	Ps. **76**; 79 2 Sam. 2. 1–11 Acts 5. 27–end
3	S G	**THE ELEVENTH SUNDAY AFTER TRINITY (Proper 13)** Track 1 Track 2 Gen. 32. 22–31 Isa. 55. 1–5 Ps. 17. 1–7 [16] Ps. 145. [8–9] 15–end Rom. 9. 1–5 Rom. 9. 1–5 Matt. 14. 13–21 Matt. 14. 13–21	Ps. 85 Song of Sol. 5. 2–end or 1 Macc. 3. 1–12 2 Pet. 1. 1–15
4 DEL 18	M G	*John-Baptiste Vianney, Curé d'Ars, Spiritual Guide, 1859* Jer. ch. 28 Ps. 119. 89–96 Matt. 14. 13–21 or 14. 22–end	Ps. **80**; 82 2 Sam. 3. 12–end Acts ch. 6
5	Tu 	**Oswald, King of Northumbria, Martyr, 642** Com. Martyr or Jer. 30. 1–2, 12–15, 18–22 esp. 1 Pet. 4. 12–end Ps. 102. 16–21 Matt. 14. 22–end or 15. 1–2, 10–14	Ps. 87; **89**. *1–18* 2 Sam. 5. 1–12 Acts 7. 1–16
	Gr		
6	W W	**THE TRANSFIGURATION OF OUR LORD** Dan. 7. 9–10, 13–14 Ps. 97 2 Pet. 1. 16–19 Luke 9. 28–36	MP: Ps. 27; 150 Ecclus. 48. 1–10 or 1 Kings 19. 1–16 1 John 3. 1–3
7	Th G	*John Mason Neale, Priest, Hymn Writer, 1866* Jer. 31. 31–34 Ps. 51. 11–18 Matt. 16. 13–23	Ps. 90; **92** 2 Sam. 7. 1–17 Acts 7. 44–53

Second Service Evening Prayer		Calendar and Holy Communion	Morning Prayer	Evening Prayer
Ps. **72**; 75 Prov. 1. 1–19 Mark 2.23 – 3.6	G		1 Sam. ch. 24 Acts 3. 11–end	Prov. 1. 1–19 Mark 2.23 – 3.6
Ps. 74 Prov. 1. 20–end Mark 3. 7–19a	G		1 Sam. ch. 26 Acts 4. 1–12	Prov. 1. 20–end Mark 3. 7–19a
Ps. 119. 81–104 Prov. ch. 2 Mark 3. 19b–end	G		1 Sam. 28. 3–end Acts 4. 13–31	Prov. ch. 2 Mark 3. 19b–end
Ps. 78. 40–end† Prov. 3. 1–26 Mark 4. 1–20	G		1 Sam. ch. 31 Acts 4.32 – 5.11	Prov. 3. 1–26 Mark 4. 1–20
Ps. 69 Prov. 3.27 – 4.19 Mark 4. 21–34	G	Lammas Day	2 Sam. ch. 1 Acts 5. 12–26	Prov. 3.27 – 4.19 Mark 4. 21–34
Ps. 81; **84** Prov. 6. 1–19 Mark 4. 35–end ct	G		2 Sam. 2. 1–11 Acts 5. 27–end	Prov. 6. 1–19 Mark 4. 35–end ct
		THE ELEVENTH SUNDAY AFTER TRINITY		
Ps. 80. 1–8 [9–end] 1 Kings 10. 1–13 Acts 13. 1–13 *Gospel:* John 6. 24–35	G	1 Kings 3. 5–15 Ps. 28 1 Cor. 15. 1–11 Luke 18. 9–14	Ps. 85 Song of Sol. 5. 2–end or 1 Macc. 3. 1–12 2 Pet. 1. 1–15	Ps. 80. 1–8 [9–end] 1 Kings 10. 1–13 Acts 13. 1–13
Ps. **85**; 86 Prov. 8. 1–21 Mark 5. 1–20	G		2 Sam. 3. 12–end Acts ch. 6	Prov. 8. 1–21 Mark 5. 1–20
Ps. 89. 19–end Prov. 8. 22–end Mark 5. 21–34 *or First EP of The Transfiguration* Ps. 99; 110 Exod. 24. 12–end John 12. 27–36a **W** ct	G		2 Sam. 5. 1–12 Acts 7. 1–16	Prov. 8. 22–end Mark 5. 21–34 *or First EP of The Transfiguration* (Ps. 99; 110) Exod. 24. 12–end John 12. 27–36a **W** ct
EP: Ps. 72 Exod. 34. 29–end 2 Cor. ch. 3	W	**THE TRANSFIGURATION OF OUR LORD** Exod. 24. 12–end Ps. 84. 1–7 1 John 3. 1–3 Mark 9. 2–7	(Ps. 27; 150) Ecclus. 48. 1–10 or 1 Kings 19. 1–16 2 Pet. 1. 16–19	(Ps. 72) Exod. 34. 29–end 2 Cor. ch. 3
Ps. 94 Prov. 10. 1–12 Mark 6. 1–13	Gw	**The Name of Jesus** Jer. 14. 7–9 Ps. 8 Acts 4. 8–12 Matt. 1. 20–23	2 Sam. 7. 1–17 Acts 7. 44–53	Prov. 10. 1–12 Mark 6. 1–13

August 2008

			Sunday Principal Service / Weekday Eucharist	Third Service / Morning Prayer
8	F		**Dominic, Priest, Founder of the Order of Preachers, 1221**	
			Com. Religious *or* Nahum 2. 1, 3; 3. 1–3, 6–7	Ps. **88**; (95)
			also Ecclus. 39. 1–10 Ps. 137. 1–6	2 Sam. 7. 18–end
			or Deut. 32. 35–36, 39, 41	Acts 7.54 – 8.3
	Gw		Matt. 16. 24–28	
9	Sa		**Mary Sumner, Founder of the Mothers' Union, 1921**	
			Com. Saint *or* Hab. 1.12 – 2.4	Ps. 96; **97**; 100
			also Heb. 13. 1–5 Ps. 9. 7–11	2 Sam. ch. 9
	Gw		Matt. 17. 14–20	Acts 8. 4–25
10	S		THE TWELFTH SUNDAY AFTER TRINITY **(Proper 14)**	
			Track 1 Track 2	
			Gen. 37. 1–4, 12–28 1 Kings 19. 9–18	Ps. 88
			Ps. 105. 1–6, 16–22, 45b (*or* 1–10) Ps. 85. 8–13	Song of Sol. 8. 5–7
			Rom. 10. 5–15 Rom. 10. 5–15	*or* 1 Macc. 14. 4–15
	G		Matt. 14. 22–33 Matt. 14. 22–33	2 Pet. 3. 8–13
11 DEL 19	M		**Clare of Assisi, Founder of the Minoresses (Poor Clares), 1253**	
			John Henry Newman, Priest, Tractarian, 1890	
			Com. Religious *or* Ezek. 1. 2–5, 24–end	Ps. **98**; 99; 101
			esp. Song of Sol. 8. 6–7 Ps. 148. 1–4, 12–13a	2 Sam. ch. 11
	Gw		Matt. 17. 22–end	Acts 8. 26–end
12	Tu		Ezek. 2.8 – 3.4	Ps. **106**† (*or* 103)
			Ps. 119. 65–72	2 Sam. 12. 1–25
	G		Matt. 18. 1–5, 10, 12–14	Acts 9. 1–19a
13	W		**Jeremy Taylor, Bishop of Down and Connor, Teacher, 1667**	
			Florence Nightingale, Nurse, Social Reformer, 1910; Octavia Hill, Social Reformer, 1912	
			Com. Teacher *or* Ezek. 9. 1–7, 10, 18–22	Ps. 110; **111**; 112
			also Titus 2. 7–8, 11–14 Ps. 113	2 Sam. 15. 1–12
	Gw		Matt. 18. 15–20	Acts 9. 19b–31
14	Th		*Maximilian Kolbe, Friar, Martyr, 1941*	
			Ezek. 12. 1–12	Ps. 113; **115**
			Ps. 78. 58–64	2 Sam. 15. 13–end
			Matt. 18.21 – 19.1	Acts 9. 32–end
	G			
15	F		THE BLESSED VIRGIN MARY*	
			Isa. 61. 10–end	MP: Ps. 98; 138; 147. 1–12
			or Rev. 11.19 – 12.6, 10	Isa. 7. 10–15
			Ps. 45. 10–end	Luke 11. 27–28
			Gal. 4. 4–7	
	W		Luke 1. 46–55	
			or, if The Blessed Virgin Mary Ezek. 16. 1–15, 60–end	Ps. 139
			is celebrated on 8 September: Ps. 118. 14–18	2 Sam. 16. 1–14
	G		Matt. 19. 3–12	Acts 10. 1–16
16	Sa		Ezek. 18. 1–10, 13, 30, 32	Ps. 120; **121**; 122
			Ps. 51. 1–3, 15–17	2 Sam. 17. 1–23
			Matt. 19. 13–15	Acts 10. 17–33
	G			
17	S		THE THIRTEENTH SUNDAY AFTER TRINITY **(Proper 15)**	
			Track 1 Track 2	
			Gen. 45. 1–15 Isa. 56. 1, 6–8	Ps. 92
			Ps. 133 Ps. 67	Jonah ch. 1
			Rom. 11. 1–2a, 29–32 Rom. 11. 1–2a, 29–32	*or* Ecclus. 3. 1–15
	G		Matt. 15. [10–20] 21–28 Matt. 15. [10–20] 21–28	2 Pet. 3. 14–end

*The Blessed Virgin Mary may be celebrated on 8 September instead of 15 August.

Second Service Evening Prayer		Calendar and Holy Communion	Morning Prayer	Evening Prayer
Ps. 102 Prov. 11. 1–12 Mark 6. 14–29	G		2 Sam. 7. 18–end Acts 7.54 – 8.3	Prov. 11. 1–12 Mark 6. 14–29
Ps. 104 Prov. 12. 10–end Mark 6. 30–44 ct	G		2 Sam. ch. 9 Acts 8. 4–25	Prov. 12. 10–end Mark 6. 30–44 ct
		THE TWELFTH SUNDAY AFTER TRINITY		
Ps. 86 1 Kings 11.41 – 12.20 Acts 14. 8–20 Gospel: John 6. 35, 41–51	G	Exod. 34. 29–end Ps. 34. 1–10 2 Cor. 3. 4–9 Mark 7. 31–37	Ps. 88 Song of Sol. 8. 5–7 or 1 Macc. 14. 4–15 2 Pet. 3. 8–13	Ps. 86 1 Kings 11.41 – 12.20 Acts 14. 8–20
Ps. **105**† (or 103) Prov. 14.31 – 15.17 Mark 6. 45–end	G		2 Sam. ch. 11 Acts 8. 26–end	Prov. 14.31 – 15.17 Mark 6. 45–end
Ps. 107† Prov. 15. 18–end Mark 7. 1–13	G		2 Sam. 12. 1–25 Acts 9. 1–19a	Prov. 15. 18–end Mark 7. 1–13
Ps. 119. 129–152 Prov. 18. 10–end Mark 7. 14–23	G		2 Sam. 15. 1–12 Acts 9. 19b–31	Prob. 18. 10–end Mark 7. 14–23
Ps. 114; **116**; 117 Prov. 20. 1–22 Mark 7. 24–30 or First EP of The Blessed Virgin Mary Ps. 72 Prov. 8. 22–31 John 19. 23–27 **W** ct	G		2 Sam. 15. 13–end Acts 9. 32–end	Prov. 20. 1–22 Mark 7. 24–30
		To celebrate The Blessed Virgin Mary, see *Common Worship* provision.		
EP: Ps. 132 Song of Sol. 2. 1–7 Acts 1. 6–14			2 Sam. 16. 1–14 Acts 10. 1–16	Prov. 22. 1–16 Mark 7. 31–end
Ps. **130**; 131; 137 Prov. 22. 1–16 Mark 7. 31–end	G			
Ps. 118 Prov. 24. 23–end Mark 8. 1–10 ct	G		2 Sam. 17. 1–23 Acts 10. 17–33	Prov. 24. 23–end Mark 8. 1–10 ct
		THE THIRTEENTH SUNDAY AFTER TRINITY		
Ps. 90. 1–12 [13–end] 2 Kings 4. 1–37 Acts 16. 1–15 Gospel: John 6. 51–58	G	Lev. 19. 13–18 Ps. 74. 20–end Gal. 3. 16–22 or Heb. 13. 1–6 Luke 10. 23b–37	Ps. 92 Jonah ch. 1 or Ecclus. 3. 1–15 2 Pet. 3. 14–end	Ps. 90. 1–2 [13–end] 2 Kings 4. 1–37 Acts 16. 1–15

August 2008

			Sunday Principal Service / Weekday Eucharist	Third Service / Morning Prayer
18 DEL 20	M		Ezek. 24. 15–24 Ps. 78. 1–8	Ps. 123; 124; 125; **126** 2 Sam. 18. 1–18
	G		Matt. 19. 16–22	Acts 10. 34–end
19	Tu		Ezek. 28. 1–10 Ps. 107. 1–3, 40, 43	Ps. **132**; 133 2 Sam 18.19 – 19.8a
	G		Matt. 19. 23–end	Acts 11. 1–18
20	W	**Bernard, Abbot of Clairvaux, Teacher, 1153** *William and Catherine Booth, Founders of the Salvation Army, 1912 and 1890* Com. Teacher or Ezek. 34. 1–11 *esp.* Rev. 19. 5–9 Ps. 23		Ps. 119. 153–end 2 Sam 19. 8b–23
	Gw		Matt. 20. 1–16	Acts 11. 19–end
21	Th		Ezek. 36. 23–28 Ps. 51. 7–12	Ps. **143**; 146 2 Sam. 19. 24–end
	G		Matt. 22. 1–14	Acts 12. 1–17
22	F		Ezek. 37. 1–14 Ps. 107. 1–8	Ps. 142; **144** 2 Sam. 23. 1–7
	G		Matt. 22. 34–40	Acts 12. 18–end
23	Sa		Ezek. 43. 1–7 Ps. 85. 7–end Matt. 23. 1–12	Ps. 147 2 Sam. ch. 24 Acts 13. 1–12

	G			
24	S	**BARTHOLOMEW THE APOSTLE** (or transferred to 25th) *The reading from Acts must be used* Isa. 43. 8–13 *as either the first or second reading* or Acts 5. 12–16		MP: Ps. 86; 117 Gen. 28. 10–17
	R	*at the Eucharist.*	Ps. 145. 1–7 Acts 5. 12–16 or 1 Cor. 4. 9–15 Luke 22. 24–30	John 1. 43–end
		or, for The Fourteenth Sunday after Trinity **(Proper 16)** Track 1 Track 2 Exod. 1.8 – 2.10 Isa. 51. 1–6 Ps. 124 Ps. 138 Rom. 12. 1–8 Rom. 12. 1–8		Ps. 104. 1–25 Jonah ch. 2 or Ecclus. 3. 17–29
	G	Matt. 16. 13–20	Matt. 16. 13–20	Rev. ch. 1
25 DEL 21	M	For Bartholomew, see 24th	2 Thess. 1. 1–5, 11–12 Ps. 39. 1–9 Matt. 23. 13–22	Ps. **1**; 2; 3 1 Kings 1. 5–31 Acts 13. 13–43
	G			
26	Tu		2 Thess. 2. 1–3a, 14–17 Ps. 98 Matt. 23. 23–26	Ps. **5**; 6; (8) 1 Kings 1.32 – 2.4, 10–12 Acts 13.44 – 14.7
	G			
27	W	**Monica, Mother of Augustine of Hippo, 387** Com. Saint or 2 Thess. 3. 6–10, 16–18 *also* Ecclus. 26. 1–3, 13–16 Ps. 128 Matt. 23. 27–32		Ps. 119. 1–32 1 Kings ch. 3 Acts 14. 8–end
	Gw			
28	Th	**Augustine, Bishop of Hippo, Teacher, 430** Com. Teacher or 1 Cor. 1. 1–9 *esp.* Ecclus. 39. 1–10 Ps. 145. 1–7 *also* Rom. 13. 11–13 Matt. 24. 42–end		Ps. 14; **15**; 16 1 Kings 4.29 – 5.12 Acts 15. 1–21
	Gw			

BOOK OF COMMON PRAYER

Second Service Evening Prayer	Calendar and Holy Communion	Morning Prayer	Evening Prayer
Ps. *127*; 128; 129 Prov. 25. 1–14 Mark 8. 11–21	G	2 Sam. 18. 1–18 Acts 10. 34–end	Prov. 25. 1–14 Mark 8. 11–21
Ps. (134); *135* Prov. 25. 15–end Mark 8. 22–26	G	2 Sam 18.19 – 19.8a Acts 11. 1–18	Prov. 25. 15–end Mark 8. 22–26
Ps. 136 Prov. 26. 12–end Mark 8.27 – 9.1	G	2 Sam 19. 8b–23 Acts 11. 19–end	Prov. 26. 12–end Mark 8.27 – 9.1
Ps. *138*; 140; 141 Prov. 27. 1–22 Mark 9. 2–13	G	2 Sam. 19. 24–end Acts 12. 1–17	Prov. 27. 1–22 Mark 9. 2–13
Ps. 145 Prov. 30. 1–9, 24–31 Mark 9. 14–29	G	2 Sam. 23. 1–7 Acts 12. 18–end	Prov. 30. 1–9, 24–31 Mark 9. 14–29
Ps. *148*; 149; 150 Prov. 31. 10–end Mark 9. 30–37 ct or First EP of Bartholomew Ps. 97 Isa. 61. 1–9 2 Cor. 6. 1–10 R ct	G	2 Sam. ch. 24 Acts 13. 1–12	Prov. 31. 10–end Mark 9. 30–37 ct or First EP of Bartholomew (Ps. 97) Isa. 61. 1–9 2 Cor. 6. 1–10 R ct
EP: Ps. 91; 116 Ecclus. 39. 1–10 or Deut. 18. 15–19 Matt. 10. 1–22	**BARTHOLOMEW THE APOSTLE** (or transferred to 25th) Gen. 28. 10–17 Ps. 15 Acts 5. 12–16 Luke 22. 24–30 R	Ps. 86; 117 Isa. 43. 8–13 John 1. 43–end	Ps. 91; 116 Ecclus. 39. 1–10 or Deut. 18. 15–19 Matt. 10. 1–22
	or, for The Fourteenth Sunday after Trinity		
Ps. 95 2 Kings 6. 8–23 Acts 17. 15–end Gospel: John 6. 56–69	2 Kings 5. 9–16 Ps. 118. 1–9 Gal. 5. 16–24 Luke 17. 11–19 G	Ps. 104. 1–25 Jonah ch. 2 or Ecclus. 3. 17–29 Rev. ch. 1	Ps. 95 2 Kings 6. 8–23 Acts 17. 15–end
	For Bartholomew, see 24th		
Ps. *4*; 7 Wisd. ch. 1 or 1 Chron. 10.1 – 11.9 Mark 9. 38–end	G	1 Kings 1. 5–31 Acts 13. 13–43	Wisd. ch. 1 or 1 Chron. 10.1 – 11.9 Mark 9. 38–end
Ps. *9*; 10† Wisd. ch. 2 or 1 Chron. ch. 13 Mark 10. 1–16	G	1 Kings 1.32 – 2.4, 10–12 Acts 13.44 – 14.7	Wisd. ch. 2 or 1 Chron. ch. 13 Mark 10. 1–16
Ps. *11*; 12; 13 Wisd. 3. 1–9 or 1 Chron. 15.1 – 16.3 Mark 10. 17–31	G	1 Kings ch. 3 Acts 14. 8–end	Wisd. 3. 1–9 or 1 Chron. 15.1 – 16.3 Mark 10. 17–31
Ps. 18† Wisd. 4. 7–end or 1 Chron. ch. 17 Mark 10. 32–34	**Augustine, Bishop of Hippo, 430** Com. Doctor Gw	1 Kings 4.29 – 5.12 Acts 15. 1–21	Wisd. 4. 7–end or 1 Chron. ch. 17 Mark 10. 32–34

COMMON WORSHIP

August 2008

			Sunday Principal Service / Weekday Eucharist	Third Service / Morning Prayer
29	F	**The Beheading of John the Baptist** Jer. 1. 4–10 Ps. 11 Heb. 11.32 – 12.2	*or* 1 Cor. 1. 17–25 Ps. 33. 6–12 Matt. 25. 1–13	Ps. 17; **19** 1 Kings 6. 1, 11–28 Acts 15. 22–35
		Gr	Matt. 14. 1–12	
30	Sa	**John Bunyan, Spiritual Writer, 1688** Com. Teacher *also* Heb. 12. 1–2 Luke 21. 21, 34–36	*or* 1 Cor. 1. 26–end Ps. 33. 12–15, 20–end Matt. 25. 14–30	Ps. 20; 21; **23** 1 Kings 8. 1–30 Acts 15.36 – 16.5
		Gw			
31	S	THE FIFTEENTH SUNDAY AFTER TRINITY **(Proper 17)** *Track 1* Exod. 3. 1–15 Ps. 105. 1–6, 23–26, 45b *or* Ps. 115 Rom. 12. 9–end	*Track 2* Jer. 15. 15–21 Ps. 26. 1–8 Rom. 12. 9–end Matt. 16. 21–end	Ps. 107. 1–32 Jonah 3. 1–9 *or* Ecclus. 11. [7–18] 19–28 Rev. 3. 14–end
		G	Matt. 16. 21–end		

September 2008

1 DEL 22	M	*Giles of Provence, Hermit, c. 710*	1 Cor. 2. 1–5 Ps. 33. 12–21 Luke 4. 16–30	Ps. 27; **30** 1 Kings 8. 31–62 Acts 16. 6–24
		G		
2	Tu	*The Martyrs of Papua New Guinea, 1901 and 1942*	1 Cor. 2. 10–end Ps. 145. 10–17 Luke 4. 31–37	Ps. 32; **36** 1 Kings 8.63 – 9. 9 Acts 16. 25–end
		G		
3	W	**Gregory the Great, Bishop of Rome, Teacher, 604** Com. Teacher *also* 1 Thess. 2. 3–8	*or* 1 Cor. 3. 1–9 Ps. 62 Luke 4. 38–end	Ps. 34 1 Kings 10. 1–25 Acts 17. 1–15
		Gw		
4	Th	*Birinus, Bishop of Dorchester (Oxon), Apostle of Wessex, 650**	1 Cor. 3. 18–end Ps. 24. 1–6 Luke 5. 1–11	Ps. 37† 1 Kings 11. 1–13 Acts 17. 16–end
		G		
5	F		1 Cor. 4. 1–5 Ps. 37. 3–8 Luke 5. 33–end	Ps. 31 1 Kings 11. 26–end Acts 18. 1 – 21
		G		
6	Sa	*Allen Gardiner, Missionary, Founder of the South American Mission Society, 1851*	1 Cor. 4. 6–15 Ps. 145. 18–end Luke 6. 1–5	Ps. 41; **42**; 43 1 Kings 12. 1–24 Acts 18.22 – 19.7
		G		
7	S	THE SIXTEENTH SUNDAY AFTER TRINITY **(Proper 18)** *Track 1* Exod. 12. 1–14 Ps. 149 Rom. 13. 8–end	*Track 2* Ezek. 33. 7–11 Ps. 119. 33–40 Rom. 13. 8–end Matt. 18. 15–20	Ps. 119. 17–32 Jonah 3.10 – 4.11 *or* Ecclus. 27.30 – 28.9 Rev. 8. 1–5
		G	Matt. 18. 15–20		
8 DEL 23	M	**The Birth of the Blessed Virgin Mary**** Com. BVM	*or* 1 Cor. 5. 1–8 Ps. 5. 5–9a Luke 6. 6–11	Ps. 44 1 Kings 12.25 – 13.10 Acts 19. 8–20
		Gw		

*Cuthbert may be celebrated on 4 September instead of 20 March, when the Common of a Missionary readings are used, *esp*. Ezek. 34. 11–16, *also* Matt. 18. 12–14.   **The Blessed Virgin Mary may be celebrated on 8 September instead of 15 August.

Second Service Evening Prayer	Calendar and Holy Communion	Morning Prayer	Evening Prayer
Ps. 22 Wisd. 5. 1–16 or 1 Chron. 21.1 – 22.1 Mark 10. 35–45	**The Beheading of John the Baptist** 2 Chron. 24. 17–21 Ps. 92. 11–end Heb. 11.32 – 12.2 Gr Matt. 14. 1–12	1 Kings 6. 1, 11–28 Acts 15. 22–35	Wisd. 5. 1–16 or 1 Chron. 21.1 – 22.1 Mark 10. 35–45
Ps. *24*; 25 Wisd. 5.17 – 6.11 or 1 Chron. 22. 2–end Mark 10. 46–end ct	G	1 Kings 8. 1–30 Acts 15.36 – 16.5	Wisd. 5.17 – 6.11 or 1 Chron. 22. 2–end Mark 10. 46–end ct
	THE FIFTEENTH SUNDAY AFTER TRINITY		
Ps. 105. 1–15 2 Kings 6. 24–25; 7. 3–end Acts 18. 1–16 Gospel: Mark 7. 1–8, 14–15, 21–23	Josh. 24. 14–25 Ps. 92. 1–6 Gal. 6. 11–end Matt. 6. 24–end G	Ps. 107. 1–32 Jonah 3. 1–9 or Ecclus. 11. [7–18] 19–28 Rev. 3. 14–end	Ps. 105. 1–15 2 Kings 6. 24–25; 7. 3–end Acts 18. 1–16
Ps. 26; *28*; 29 Wisd. 6. 12–23 or 1 Chron. 28. 1–10 Mark 11. 1–11	**Giles of Provence, Hermit, c. 710** Com. Abbot Gw	1 Kings 8. 31–62 Acts 16. 6–24	Wisd. 6. 12–23 or 1 Chron. 28. 1–10 Mark 11. 1–11
Ps. 33 Wisd. 7. 1–14 or 1 Chron. 28. 11–end Mark 11. 12–26	G	1 Kings 8.63 – 9. 9 Acts 16. 25–end	Wisd. 7. 1–14 or 1 Chron. 28. 11–end Mark 11. 12–26
Ps. 119. 33–56 Wisd. 7.15 – 8.4 or 1 Chron. 29. 1–9 Mark 11. 27–end	G	1 Kings 10. 1–25 Acts 17. 1–15	Wisd. 7.15 – 8.4 or 1 Chron. 29. 1–9 Mark 11. 27–end
Ps. 39; *40* Wisd. 8. 5–18 or 1 Chron. 29. 10–20 Mark 12. 1–12	G	1 Kings 11. 1–13 Acts 17. 16–end	Wisd. 8. 5–15 or 1 Chron. 29. 10–20 Mark 12. 1–12
Ps. 35 Wisd. 8.21 – 9.end or 1 Chron. 29. 21–end Mark 12. 13–17	G	1 Kings 11.26–end Acts 18. 1–21	Wisd. 8.21 – 9.end or 1 Chron. 29. 21–end Mark 12. 13–17
Ps. 45; *46* Wisd. 10.15 – 11.10 or 2 Chron. 1. 1–13 Mark 12. 18–27 ct	G	1 Kings 12. 1–24 Acts 18.22 – 19.7	Wisd. 10.15 – 11.10 or 2 Chron. 1. 1–13 Mark 12. 18–27 ct
	THE SIXTEENTH SUNDAY AFTER TRINITY		
Ps. 108; [115] Ezek. 12.21 – 13.16 Acts 19. 1–20 Gospel: Mark 7. 24–37	1 Kings 17. 17–end Ps. 102. 12–17 Eph. 3. 13–end G Luke 7. 11–17	Ps. 119. 17–32 Jonah 3.10 – 4.11 or Ecclus. 27.30 – 28.9 Rev. 8. 1–5	Ps. 108; [115] Ezek. 12.21 – 13.16 Mark 7. 24–30
Ps. *47*; 49 Wisd. 11.21 – 12.2 or 2 Chron. 2. 1–16 Mark 12. 28–34	**The Nativity of the Blessed Virgin Mary** Gen. 3. 9–15 Ps. 45. 11–18 Rom. 5. 12–17 Gw Luke 11. 27–28	1 Kings 12.25 – 13.10 Acts 19. 8–20	Wisd. 11.21 – 12.2 or 2 Chron. 2. 1–16 Mark 12. 28–34

September 2008

			Sunday Principal Service / Weekday Eucharist	Third Service / Morning Prayer
9	Tu G	Charles Fuge Lowder, Priest, 1880	1 Cor. 6. 1–11 Ps. 149. 1–5 Luke 6. 12–19	Ps. **48**; 52 1 Kings 13. 11–end Acts 19. 21–end
10	W G		1 Cor. 7. 25–31 Ps. 45. 11–end Luke 6. 20–26	Ps. 119. 57–80 1 Kings ch. 17 Acts 20. 1–16
11	Th G		1 Cor. 8. 1–7, 11–end Ps. 139. 1–9 Luke 6. 27–38	Ps. 56; **57**; (63†) 1 Kings 18. 1–20 Acts 20. 17–end
12	F G		1 Cor. 9. 16–19, 22–end Ps. 84. 1–6 Luke 6. 39–42	Ps. **51**; 54 1 Kings 18. 21–end Acts 21. 1–16
13	Sa	**John Chrysostom, Bishop of Constantinople, Teacher, 407** Com. Teacher or *esp.* Matt. 5. 13–19 *also* Jer. 1. 4–10	1 Cor. 10. 14–22 Ps. 116. 10–end Luke 6. 43–end	Ps. 68 1 Kings ch. 19 Acts 21. 17–36
14	S R	Gw HOLY CROSS DAY (or transferred to 15th)	Num. 21. 4–9 Ps. 22. 23–28 Phil. 2. 6–11 John 3. 13–17	*MP*: Ps. 2; 8; 146 Gen. 3. 1–15 John 12. 27–36a
		or, for The Seventeenth Sunday after Trinity (Proper 19): Track 1 Exod. 14. 19–end Ps. 114 *or Canticle:* Exod. 15. 1b–11, 20–21 Rom. 14. 1–12	Track 2 Gen. 50. 15–21 Ps. 103. [1–7] 8–13 Rom. 14. 1–12 Matt. 18. 21–35	Ps. 119. 65–88 Isa. 44.24 – 45.8 Rev. 12. 1–12
	G	Matt. 18. 21–35		
15 DEL 24	M Gr	For Holy Cross Day, see 14th **Cyprian, Bishop of Carthage, Martyr, 258** Com. Martyr or *esp.* 1 Pet. 4. 12–end *also* Matt. 18. 18–22	1 Cor. 11. 17–26, 33 Ps. 40. 7–11 Luke 7. 1–10	Ps. 71 1 Kings ch. 21 Acts 21.37 – 22.21
16	Tu Gw	**Ninian, Bishop of Galloway, Apostle of the Picts, c. 432** *Edward Bouverie Pusey, Priest, Tractarian, 1882* Com. Missionary or *esp.* Acts 13. 46–49 Mark 16. 15–end	1 Cor. 12. 12–14, 27–end Ps. 100 Luke 7. 11–17	Ps. 73 1 Kings 22. 1–28 Acts 22.22 – 23.11
17	W Gw	**Hildegard, Abbess of Bingen, Visionary, 1179** Com. Religious or *also* 1 Cor. 2. 9–13 Luke 10. 21–24	1 Cor. 12.31b – 13.end Ps. 33. 1–12 Luke 7. 31–35	Ps. 77 1 Kings 22. 29–45 Acts 23. 12–end

BOOK OF COMMON PRAYER

Second Service Evening Prayer	Calendar and Holy Communion	Morning Prayer	Evening Prayer
Ps. 50 Wisd. 12. 12–21 or 2 Chron. ch. 3 Mark 12. 35–end	G	1 Kings 13. 11–end Acts 19. 21–end	Wisd. 12. 12–21 or 2 Chron. ch. 3 Mark 12. 35–end
Ps. 59; 60; (67) Wisd. 13. 1–9 or 2 Chron. ch. 5 Mark 13. 1–13	G	1 Kings ch. 17 Acts 20. 1–16	Wisd. 13. 1–9 or 2 Chron. ch. 5 Mark 13. 1–13
Ps. 61; 62; 64 Wisd. 16.15 – 17.1 or 2 Chron. 6. 1–21 Mark 13. 14–23	G	1 Kings 18. 1–20 Acts 20. 17–end	Wisd. 16.15 – 17.1 or 2 Chron. 6. 1–21 Mark 13. 14–23
Ps. 38 Wisd. 18. 6–19 or 2 Chron. 6. 22–end Mark 13. 24–31	G	1 Kings 18. 21–end Acts 21. 1–16	Wisd. 18. 6–19 or 2 Chron. 6. 22–end Mark 13. 24–31
Ps. 65; 66 Wisd. ch. 19 or 2 Chron. ch. 7 Mark 13. 32–end ct or First EP of Holy Cross Day Ps. 66 Isa. 52.13 – 53.end Eph. 2. 11–end R ct	G	1 Kings ch. 19 Acts 21. 17–36	Wisd. ch. 19 or 2 Chron. ch. 7 Mark 13. 32–end ct
EP: Ps. 110; 150 Isa. 63. 1–16 1 Cor. 1. 18–25 Ps. 119. 41–48 [49–64] Ezek. 20. 1–8, 33–44 Acts 20. 17–end Gospel: Mark 8. 27–38	**THE SEVENTEENTH SUNDAY AFTER TRINITY** Prov. 25. 6–14 Ps. 33. 6–12 Eph. 4. 1–6 Luke 14. 1–11 G	Ps. 119. 65–88 Isa. 44.24 – 45.8 Rev. 12. 1–12	Ps. 119. 41–48 [49–64] Ezek. 20. 1–8, 33–44 Acts 20. 17–end
Ps. 72; 75 1 Macc. 1. 1–19 or 2 Chron. 9. 1–12 Mark 14. 1–11	G	1 Kings ch. 21 Acts 21.37 – 22.21	1 Macc. 1. 1–19 or 2 Chron. 9. 1–12 Mark 14. 1–11
Ps. 74 1 Macc. 1. 20–40 or 2 Chron. 10.1 – 11.4 Mark 14. 12–25	G	1 Kings 22. 1–28 Acts 22.22 – 23.11	1 Macc. 1. 20–40 or 2 Chron. 10.1 – 11.4 Mark 14. 12–25
Ps. 119. 81–104 1 Macc. 1. 41–end or 2 Chron. ch. 12 Mark 14. 26–42	**Lambert, Bishop of Maastricht, Martyr, 709** Com. Martyr Gr	1 Kings 22. 29–45 Acts 23. 12–end	1 Macc. 1. 41–end or 2 Chron. ch. 12 Mark 14. 26–42

September 2008

			Sunday Principal Service / Weekday Eucharist	Third Service / Morning Prayer
18	Th G		1 Cor. 15. 1–11 Ps. 118. 1–2, 17–20 Luke 7. 36–end	Ps. 78. 1–39† 2 Kings 1. 2–17 Acts 24. 1–23
19	F G	Theodore of Tarsus, Archbishop of Canterbury, 690 1 Cor. 15. 12–20 Ps. 17. 1–8 Luke 8. 1–3		Ps. 55 2 Kings 2. 1–18 Acts 24.24 – 25.12
20	Sa Gr	**John Coleridge Patteson, first Bishop of Melanesia, and his Companions, Martyrs, 1871** Com. Martyr *esp.* 2 Chron. 24. 17–21 *also* Acts 7. 55–end	or	1 Cor. 15. 35–37, 42–49 Ps. 30. 1–5 Luke 8. 4–15	Ps. **76**; 79 2 Kings 4. 1–37 Acts 25. 13–end

21	S R	**MATTHEW, APOSTLE AND EVANGELIST** (or transferred to 22nd) Prov. 3. 13–18 Ps. 119. 65–72 2 Cor. 4. 1–6 Matt. 9. 9–13			MP: Ps. 49; 117 1 Kings 19. 15–end 2 Tim. 3. 14–end
		or, for the Eighteenth Sunday after Trinity (Proper 20): Track 1 Exod. 16. 2–15 Ps. 105. [1–6] 37–45 Phil. 1. 21–end Matt. 20. 1–16		Track 2 Jonah 3.10 – 4.end Ps. 145. 1–8 Phil. 1. 21–end Matt. 20. 1–16	Ps. 119. 153–176 Isa. 45. 9–22 Rev. 14. 1–5
	G				
22 DEL 25	M G			Prov. 3. 27–34 Ps. 15 Luke 8. 16–18	Ps. **80**; 82 2 Kings ch. 5 Acts 26. 1–23
23	Tu G			Prov. 21. 1–6, 10–13 Ps. 119. 1–8 Luke 8. 19–21	Ps. 87; **89. 1–18** 2 Kings 6. 1–23 Acts 26. 24–end
24	W G or R	Ember Day* Prov. 30. 5–9 Ps. 119. 105–112 Luke 9. 1–6			Ps. 119. 105–128 2 Kings 9. 1–16 Acts 27. 1–26
25	Th Gw	**Lancelot Andrewes, Bishop of Winchester, Spiritual Writer, 1626** Sergei of Radonezh, Russian Monastic Reformer, Teacher, 1392 Com. Bishop *esp.* Isa. 6. 1–8	or	Eccles. 1. 2–11 Ps. 90. 1–6 Luke 9. 7–9	Ps. 90; **92** 2 Kings 9. 17–end Acts 27. 27–end
26	F G or R	Ember Day* Wilson Carlile, Founder of the Church Army, 1942 Eccles. 3. 1–11 Ps. 144. 1–4 Luke 9. 18–22			Ps. **88**; (95) 2 Kings 12. 1–19 Acts 28. 1–16

*For Ember Day provision, see p. 13.

BOOK OF COMMON PRAYER

Second Service Evening Prayer	Calendar and Holy Communion	Morning Prayer	Evening Prayer
Ps. 78. 40–end† 1 Macc. 2. 1–28 *or* 2 Chron. 13.1 – 14.1 Mark 14. 43–52	G	2 Kings 1. 2–17 Acts 24. 1–23	1 Macc. 2. 1–28 *or* 2 Chron. 13.1 – 14.1 Mark 14. 43–52
Ps. 69 1 Macc. 2. 29–48 *or* 2 Chron. 14. 2–end Mark 14. 53–65	G	2 Kings 2. 1–18 Acts 24.24 – 25.12	1 Macc. 2. 29–48 *or* 2 Chron. 14. 2–end Mark 14. 53–65
Ps. 81; **84** 1 Macc. 2. 49–end *or* 2 Chron. 15. 1–15 Mark 14. 66–end ct *or First EP of Matthew* Ps. 34 Isa. 33. 13–17 Matt. 6. 19–end **R** ct	G	2 Kings 4. 1–37 Acts 25. 13–end	1 Macc. 2. 49–end *or* 2 Chron. 15. 1–15 Mark 14. 66–end ct *or First EP of Matthew* (Ps. 34) Prov. 3. 3–18 Matt. 6. 19–end **R** ct
EP: Ps. 119. 33–40, 89–96 Eccles. 5. 4–12 Matt. 19. 16–end	**MATTHEW, APOSTLE AND EVANGELIST** (or transferred to 22nd) Isa. 33. 13–17 Ps. 119. 65–72 2 Cor. 4. 1–6 Matt. 9. 9–13 *or, for the Eighteenth Sunday after Trinity:* R	Ps. 49; 117 1 Kings 19. 15–end 2 Tim. 3. 14–end	Ps. 119. 33–40, 89–96 Eccles. 5. 4–12 Matt. 19. 16–end
Ps. 119. [113–120] 121–128 [129–136] Ezek. 33.23, 30 – 34.10 Acts 26.1, 9–25, *Gospel:* Mark 9. 30–37	Deut. 6. 4–9 Ps. 122 1 Cor. 1. 4–8 Matt. 22. 34–end G	Ps. 119. 153–176 Isa. 45. 9–22 Rev. 14. 1–5	Ps. 119. [113–120] 121–128 [129–136] Ezek. 33.23, 30 – 34.10 Acts 26.1, 9–25
Ps. **85**; 86 1 Macc. 3. 1–26 *or* 2 Chron. 17. 1–12 Mark 15. 1–15	G	2 Kings ch. 5 Acts 26. 1–23	1 Macc. 3. 1–26 *or* 2 Chron. 17. 1–12 Mark 15. 1–15
Ps. 89. 19–end 1 Macc. 3. 27–41 *or* 2 Chron. 18. 1–27 Mark 15. 16–32	G	2 Kings 6. 1–23 Acts 26. 24–end	1 Macc. 3. 27–41 *or* 2 Chron. 18. 1–27 Mark 15. 16–32
Ps. 91; **93** 1 Macc. 3. 42–end *or* 2 Chron. 18.28 – 19.end Mark 15. 33–41	Ember Day Ember CEG G *or* R	2 Kings 9. 1–16 Acts 27. 1–26	1 Macc. 3. 42–end *or* 2 Chron. 18.28 – 19.end Mark 15. 33–41
Ps. 94 1 Macc. 4. 1–25 *or* 2 Chron. 20. 1–23 Mark 15. 42–end	G	2 Kings 9. 17–end Acts 27. 27–end	1 Macc. 4. 1–25 *or* 2 Chron. 20. 1–23 Mark 15. 42–end
Ps. 102 1 Macc. 4. 26–35 *or* 2 Chron. 22.10 – 23.end Mark 16. 1–8	**Cyprian, Bishop of Carthage, Martyr, 258** Ember Day Ember CEG *or* Com. Martyr Gr *or* **R**	2 Kings 12. 1–19 Acts 28. 1–16	1 Macc. 4. 26–35 *or* 2 Chron. 22.10 – 23.end Mark 16. 1–8

September 2008

			Sunday Principal Service / Weekday Eucharist	Third Service / Morning Prayer

27 Sa **Vincent de Paul, Founder of the Congregation of the Mission (Lazarists), 1660**
Ember Day*
Com. Religious *or* Eccles. 11.9 – 12.8
also 1 Cor. 1. 25–end   Ps. 90. 1–2, 12–end
Matt. 25. 34–40   Luke 9. 43–45

Ps. 96; **97**; 100
2 Kings 17. 1–23
Acts 28. 17–end

Gw or **Rw**

28 S **THE NINETEENTH SUNDAY AFTER TRINITY (Proper 21)**
Track 1   Track 2
Exod. 17. 1–7   Ezek. 18. 1–4, 25–end
Ps. 78. 1–4, 12–16 (or 1–7)   Ps. 25. 1–8
Phil. 2. 1–13   Phil. 2. 1–13
Matt. 21. 23–32   Matt. 21. 23–32

Ps. 125; 126; 127
Isa. 48. 12–21
Luke 11. 37–54

G

29 M **MICHAEL AND ALL ANGELS**
DEL 26 The reading from Revelation must be used as either the first or second reading at the Eucharist.
Gen. 28. 10–17
or Rev. 12. 7–12
Ps. 103. 19–end
Rev. 12. 7–12
or Heb. 1. 5–end
John 1. 47–end

MP: Ps. 34; 150
Tobit 12. 6–end
or Dan. 12. 1–4
Acts 12. 1–11

W

30 Tu Jerome, Translator of the Scriptures, Teacher, 420
Job 3. 1–3, 11–17, 20–23
Ps. 88. 14–19
Luke 9. 51–56

Ps. **106**† (or 103)
2 Kings 18. 1–12
Phil. 1. 12–end

G

October 2008

1 W Remigius, Bishop of Rheims, Apostle of the Franks, 533; Anthony Ashley Cooper, Earl of Shaftesbury, Social Reformer, 1885
Job 9. 1–12, 14–16
Ps. 88. 1–6, 11
Luke 9. 57–end

110; **111**; 112
2 Kings 18. 13–end
Phil. 2. 1–13

G

2 Th
Job 19. 21–27a
Ps. 27. 13–16
Luke 10. 1–12

Ps. 113; **115**
2 Kings 19. 1–19
Phil. 2. 14–end

G

3 F
Job 38. 1, 12–21; 40. 3–5
Ps. 139. 6–11
Luke 10. 13–16

Ps. 139
2 Kings 19. 20–36
Phil. 3.1 – 4.1

G

4 Sa **Francis of Assisi, Friar, Deacon, Founder of the Friars Minor, 1226**
Com. Religious *or* Job 42. 1–3, 6, 12–end
also Gal. 6. 14–end   Ps. 119. 169–end
Luke 12. 22–34   Luke 10. 17–24

Ps. 120; **121**; 122
2 Kings ch. 20
Phil. 4. 2–end

Gw

*For Ember Day provision, see p. 13.

BOOK OF COMMON PRAYER

Second Service Evening Prayer	Calendar and Holy Communion	Morning Prayer	Evening Prayer
Ps. 104 1 Macc. 4. 36–end or 2 Chron. 24. 1–22 Mark 16. 9–end ct	Ember Day Ember CEG **G** or **R**	2 Kings 17. 1–23 Acts 28. 17–end	1 Macc. 4. 36–end or 2 Chron. 24. 1–22 Mark 16. 9–end ct
	THE NINETEENTH SUNDAY AFTER TRINITY		
Ps. [120; 123]; 124 Ezek. 37. 15–end 1 John 2. 22–end *Gospel:* Mark 9. 38–50 or *First EP of Michael and All Angels* Ps. 91 2 Kings 6. 8–17 Matt. 18. 1–6, 10 **W** ct	Gen. 18. 23–32 Ps. 141. 1–9 Eph. 4. 17–end Matt. 9. 1–8 **G**	Ps. 125; 126; 127 Isa. 48. 12–21 Luke 11. 37–54	Ps. [120; 123]; 124 Ezek. 37. 15–end 1 John 2. 22–end or *First EP of Michael and All Angels* Ps. 91 2 Kings 6. 8–17 John 1. 47–51 **W** ct
EP: Ps. 138; 148 Dan. 10. 4–end Rev. ch. 5	**MICHAEL AND ALL ANGELS** Dan. 10. 10–19a Ps. 103. 17–22 Rev. 12. 7–12 Matt. 18. 1–10 **W**	(Ps. 34; 150) Tobit 12. 6–end or Dan. 12. 1–4 Acts 12. 1–11	(Ps. 138; 148) Gen. 28. 10–17 Rev. ch. 5
Ps. 107† 1 Macc. 6. 18–47 or 2 Chron. ch. 28 John 13. 12–20	**G**	2 Kings 18. 1–12 Phil. 1. 12–end	1 Macc. 6. 18–47 or 2 Chron. ch. 28 John 13. 12–20
	Remigius, Bishop of Rheims, Apostle of the Franks, 533		
Ps. 119. 129–152 1 Macc. 7. 1–20 or 2 Chron. 29. 1–19 John 13. 21–30	Com. Bishop **Gw**	2 Kings 18. 13–end Phil. 2. 1–13	1 Macc. 7. 1–20 or 2 Chron. 29. 1–19 John 13. 21–30
Ps. 114; *116*; 117 1 Macc. 7. 21–end or 2 Chron. 29. 20–end John 13. 31–end	**G**	2 Kings 19. 1–19 Phil. 2. 14 – end	1 Macc. 7. 21–end or 2 Chron. 29. 20–end John 13. 31–end
Ps. *130*; 131; 137 1 Macc. 9. 1–22 or 2 Chron. ch. 30 John 14. 1–14	**G**	2 Kings 19. 20–36 Phil. 3.1 – 4.1	1 Macc. 9. 1–22 or 2 Chron. ch. 30 John 14. 1–14
Ps. 118 1 Macc. 13. 41–end; 14. 4–15 or 2 Chron. 32. 1–22 John 14. 15–end ct or *First EP of Dedication Festival* Ps. 24 2 Chron. 7. 11–16 John 4. 19–29 ℟ ct	**G**	2 Kings ch. 20 Phil. 4. 2–end	1 Macc. 13. 41–end; 14. 4–15 or 2 Chron. 32. 1–22 John 14. 15–end ct or *First EP of Dedication Festival* Ps. 24 2 Chron. 7. 11–16 John 4. 19–29 ℟ ct

October 2008

| | | Sunday Principal Service / Weekday Eucharist | Third Service / Morning Prayer |

5 S — **THE TWENTIETH SUNDAY AFTER TRINITY (Proper 22)**
Track 1
Exod. 20. 1–4, 7–9, 12–20
Ps. 19. [1–6] 7–end
Phil. 3. 4b–14
G   Matt. 21. 33–end

Track 2
Isa. 5. 1–7
Ps. 80. 8–15
Phil. 3. 4b–14
Matt. 21. 33–end

Ps. 128; 129; 134
Isa. 49. 13–23
Luke 12. 1–12

or, if observed as Dedication Festival:
1 Kings 8. 22–30
or Rev. 21. 9–14
Ps. 122
Heb. 12. 18–24
Matt. 21. 12–16

MP: Ps. 48; 150
Hag. 2. 6–9
Heb. 10. 19–25

🌙

6 M — DEL 27
William Tyndale, Translator of the Scriptures, Reformation Martyr, 1536
Com. Martyr   *or*   Gal. 1. 6–12
also Prov. 8. 4–11   Ps. 111. 1–6
2 Tim. 3. 12–end   Luke 10. 25–37
Gr

Ps. 123; 124; 125; *126*
2 Kings 21. 1–18
1 Tim. 1. 1–17

7 Tu
Gal. 1. 13–end
Ps. 139. 1–9
Luke 10. 38–end
G

Ps. *132*; 133
2 Kings 22.1–23.3
1 Tim. 1.18 – 2.end

8 W
Gal. 2. 1–2, 7–14
Ps. 117
Luke 11. 1–4
G

Ps. 119. 153–end
2 Kings 23. 4–25
1 Tim. ch. 3

9 Th
Denys, Bishop of Paris, and his Companions, Martyrs, c. 250; Robert Grosseteste, Bishop of Lincoln, Philosopher, Scientist, 1253
Gal. 3. 1–5
Canticle: Benedictus
Luke 11. 5–13
G

Ps. *143*; 146
2 Kings. 23.36 – 24.17
1 Tim. ch. 4

10 F
Paulinus, Bishop of York, Missionary, 644
Thomas Traherne, Poet, Spiritual Writer, 1674
Com. Missionary   *or*   Gal. 3. 7–14
esp. Matt. 28. 16–end   Ps. 111. 4–end
Luke 11. 15–26
Gw

Ps. 142; *144*
2 Kings 24.18 – 25.12
1 Tim. 5. 1–16

11 Sa
Ethelburga, Abbess of Barking, 675; James the Deacon, Companion of Paulinus, 7th century
Gal. 3. 22–end
Ps. 105. 1–7
Luke 11. 27–28
G

Ps. 147
2 Kings 25. 22–end
1 Tim. 5. 17–end

12 S — **THE TWENTY-FIRST SUNDAY AFTER TRINITY (Proper 23)**
Track 1
Exod. 32. 1–14
Ps. 106. 1–6 [19–23]
Phil. 4. 1–9
G   Matt. 22. 1–14

Track 2
Isa. 25. 1–9
Ps. 23
Phil. 4. 1–9
Matt. 22. 1–14

Ps. 138; 141
Isa. 50. 4–10
Luke 13. 22–30

13 M — DEL 28
Edward the Confessor, King of England, 1066
Com. Saint   *or*   Gal. 4. 21–24, 26–27, 31; 5. 1
also 2 Sam. 23. 1–5   Ps. 113
1 John 4. 13–16   Luke 11. 29–32
Gw

Ps. *1*; 2; 3
Judith ch. 4
or Exod. 22. 21–27
1 Tim. 6. 1–10

14 Tu
Gal. 5. 1–6
Ps. 119. 41–48
Luke 11. 37–41
G

Ps. *5*; 6; (8)
Judith 5.1 – 6.4
or Exod. 29.38 – 30.16
1 Tim. 6. 11–end

BOOK OF COMMON PRAYER

Second Service Evening Prayer		Calendar and Holy Communion	Morning Prayer	Evening Prayer
		THE TWENTIETH SUNDAY AFTER TRINITY		
Ps. 136. 1–9 [10–end] Prov. 2. 1–11 1 John 2. 1–17 Gospel: Mark 10. 2–16	G	Prov. 9. 1–6 Ps. 145. 15–end Eph. 5. 15–21 Matt. 22. 1–14	Ps. 128; 129; 134 Isa. 49. 13–23 Luke 12. 1–12	Ps. 136. 1–9 [10–end] Prov. 2. 1–11 1 John 2. 1–17
EP: Ps. 132 Jer. 7. 1–11 1 Cor. 3. 9–17 Gospel: Luke 19. 1–10	⅏	*or, if observed as Dedication Festival:* 2 Chron. 7. 11–16 Ps. 122 1 Cor. 3. 9–17 *or* 1 Pet. 2. 1–5 Matt. 21. 12–16 *or* John 10. 22–29	Ps. 48; 150 Hag. 2. 6–9 Heb. 10. 19–25	Ps. 132 Jer. 7. 1–11 Luke 19. 1–10
		Faith of Aquitaine, Martyr, c. 304		
Ps. *127*; 128; 129 2 Macc. 4. 7–17 *or* 2 Chron. 33. 1–13 John 15. 1–11	Gr	Com. Virgin Martyr	2 Kings 21. 1–18 1 Tim. 1. 1–17	2 Macc. 4. 7–17 *or* 2 Chron. 33. 1–13 John 15. 1–11
Ps. (134); *135* 2 Macc. 6. 12–end *or* 2 Chron. 34. 1–18 John 15. 12–17	G		2 Kings 22.1 – 23.3 1 Tim. 1.18 – 2.end	2 Macc. 6. 12–end *or* 2 Chron. 34. 1–18 John 15. 12–17
Ps. 136 2 Macc. 7. 1–19 *or* 2 Chron. 34. 19–end John 15. 18–end	G		2 Kings 23. 4–25 1 Tim. ch. 3	2 Macc. 7. 1–19 *or* 2 Chron. 34. 19–end John 15. 18–end
		Denys, Bishop of Paris, Martyr, c. 250		
Ps. *138*; 140; 141 2 Macc. 7. 20–41 *or* 2 Chron. 35. 1–19 John 16. 1–15	Gr	Com. Martyr	2 Kings. 23.36 – 24.17 1 Tim. ch. 4	2 Macc. 7. 20–41 *or* 2 Chron. 35. 1–19 John 16. 1–15
Ps. 145 Tobit ch. 1 *or* 2 Chron. 35.20 – 36.10 John 16. 16–22	G		2 Kings 24.18 – 25.12 1 Tim. 5. 1–16	Tobit ch. 1 *or* 2 Chron. 35.20 – 36.10 John 16. 16–22
Ps. *148*; 149; 150 Tobit ch. 2 *or* 2 Chron. 36. 11–end John 16. 23–end ct	G		2 Kings 25. 22–end 1 Tim. 5. 17–end	Tobit ch. 2 *or* 2 Chron. 36. 11–end John 16. 23–end ct
		THE TWENTY-FIRST SUNDAY AFTER TRINITY		
Ps. 139. 1–11 [12–18] Prov. 3. 1–18 1 John 3. 1–15 Gospel: Mark 10. 17–31	G	Gen. 32. 24–29 Ps. 90. 1–12 Eph. 6. 10–20 John 4. 46b–end	Ps. 138; 141 Isa. 50. 4–10 Luke 13. 22–30	Ps. 139. 1–11 [12–18] Prov. 3. 1–18 1 John 3. 1–15
		Edward the Confessor, King of England, 1066, translated 1163		
Ps. *4*; 7 Tobit ch. 3 *or* Micah 1. 1–9 John 17. 1–5	Gw	Com. Saint	Judith ch. 4 *or* Exod. 22. 21–27 1 Tim. 6. 1–10	Tobit ch. 3 *or* Micah 1. 1–9 John 17. 1–5
Ps. *9*; 10† Tobit ch. 4 *or* Micah ch. 2 John 17. 6–19	G		Judith 5.1 – 6.4 *or* Exod. 29.38 – 30.16 1 Tim. 6. 11–end	Tobit ch. 4 *or* Micah ch. 2 John 17. 6–19

October 2008

		Sunday Principal Service / Weekday Eucharist	Third Service / Morning Prayer
15	W Gw	**Teresa of Avila, Teacher, 1582** Com. Teacher *or* Gal. 5. 18–end *also* Rom. 8. 22–27 Ps. 1 Luke 11. 42–46	Ps. 119. 1–32 Judith 6.10 – 7.7 *or* Lev. ch. 8 2 Tim. 1. 1–14

16	Th
	G
		Nicholas Ridley, Bishop of London, and Hugh Latimer, Bishop of Worcester, Reformation Martyrs, 1555
		                                Eph. 1. 1, 3–10
		                                Ps. 98. 1–4
		                                Luke 11. 47–end
			Ps. 14; **15**; 16
			Judith 7. 19–end
			or Lev. ch. 9
			2 Tim. 1.15 – 2.13

17	F Gr	**Ignatius, Bishop of Antioch, Martyr, c. 107** Com. Martyr *or* Eph. 1. 11–14 *also* Phil. 3. 7–12 Ps. 33. 1–6, 12 John 6. 52–58 Luke 12. 1–7	Ps. 17; **19** Judith 8. 9–end *or* Lev. 16. 2–24 2 Tim. 2. 14–end

18	Sa
	
	R
		LUKE THE EVANGELIST
		                                Isa. 35. 3–6
		                                or Acts 16. 6–12a
		                                Ps. 147. 1–7
		                                2 Tim. 4. 5–17
		                                Luke 10. 1–9
			MP: Ps. 145; 146
			Isa. ch. 55
			Luke 1. 1–4

19	S G	**THE TWENTY-SECOND SUNDAY AFTER TRINITY (Proper 24)** Track 1 Track 2 Exod. 33. 12–end Isa. 45. 1–7 Ps. 99 Ps. 96. 1–9 [10–13] 1 Thess. 1. 1–10 1 Thess. 1. 1–10 Matt. 22. 15–22 Matt. 22. 15–22	Ps. 145; 149 Isa. 54. 1–14 Luke 13. 31–end
20 DEL 29	M G	Eph. 2. 1–10 Ps. 100 Luke 12. 13–21	Ps. 27; **30** Judith ch. 10 *or* Lev. 19. 1–18, 30–end 2 Tim. 4. 1–8
21	Tu G	Eph. 2. 12–end Ps. 85. 7–end Luke 12. 35–38	Ps. 32; **36** Judith ch. 11 *or* Lev. 23. 1–22 2 Tim. 4. 9–end
22	W G	Eph. 3. 2–12 Ps. 98 Luke 12. 39–48	Ps. 34 Judith ch. 12 *or* Lev. 23. 23–end Titus ch. 1
23	Th G	Eph. 3. 14–end Ps. 33. 1–6 Luke 12. 49–53	Ps. 37† Judith ch. 13 *or* Lev. 24. 1–9 Titus ch. 2
24	F G	Eph. 4. 1–6 Ps. 24. 1–6 Luke 12. 54–end	Ps. 31 Judith 15. 1–13 *or* Lev. 25. 1–24 Titus ch. 3

25	Sa
	
	G
		Crispin and Crispinian, Martyrs at Rome, c. 287
		                                  Eph. 4. 7–16
		                                  Ps. 122
		                                  Luke 13. 1–9
			Ps. 41; **42**; 43
			Judith 15.14 – 16.end
			or Num. 6. 1–5, 21–end
			Philemon

BOOK OF COMMON PRAYER

Second Service Evening Prayer	Calendar and Holy Communion	Morning Prayer	Evening Prayer
Ps. *11*; 12; 13 Tobit 5.1 – 6.1a *or* Micah ch. 3 John 17. 20–end	G	Judith 6.10 – 7.7 *or* Lev. ch. 8 2 Tim. 1. 1–14	Tobit 5.1 – 6.1a *or* Micah ch. 3 John 17. 20–end
Ps. 18† Tobit 6. 1b–end *or* Micah 4.1 – 5.1 John 18. 1–11	G	Judith 7. 19–end *or* Lev. ch. 9 2 Tim. 1.15 – 2.13	Tobit 6. 1b–end *or* Micah 4.1 – 5.1 John 18. 1–11
Ps. 22 Tobit ch. 7 *or* Micah 5. 2–end John 18. 12–27 *or First EP of Luke* Ps. 33 Hos. 6. 1–3 2 Tim. 3. 10–end **R** ct	**Etheldreda, Abbess of Ely, 679** Com. Abbess Gw	Judith 8. 9–end *or* Lev. 16. 2–24 2 Tim. 2. 14–end	Tobit ch. 7 *or* Micah 5. 2–end John 18. 12–27 *or First EP of Luke* (Ps. 33) Hos. 6. 1–3 2 Tim. 3. 10–end **R** ct
EP: Ps. 103 Ecclus. 38. 1–14 *or* Isa. 61. 1–6 Col. 4. 7–end	**LUKE THE EVANGELIST** Isa. 35. 3–6 Ps. 147. 1–6 2 Tim. 4. 5–15 Luke 10. 1–9 *or* Luke 7. 36–50 R	(Ps. 145; 146) Isa. ch. 55 Luke 1. 1–4	(Ps. 103) Ecclus. 38. 1–14 *or* Isa. 61. 1–6 Col. 4. 7–end
Ps. 142 [143. 1–11] Prov. 4. 1–18 1 John 3.16 – 4.6 Gospel: Mark 10. 35–45	**THE TWENTY-SECOND SUNDAY AFTER TRINITY** Gen. 45. 1–7, 15 Ps. 133 Phil. 1. 3–11 Matt. 18. 21–end G	Ps. 138 Isa. 54. 1–14 Luke 13. 31–end	Ps. 142 [143. 1–11] Prov. 4. 1–18 1 John 3.16 – 4.6
Ps. 26; *28*; 29 Tobit ch. 9 *or* Micah 7. 1–7 John 19. 1–16	G	Judith ch. 10 *or* Lev. 19. 1–18, 30–end 2 Tim. 4. 1–8	Tobit ch. 9 *or* Micah 7. 1–7 John 19. 1–16
Ps. 33 Tobit ch. 10 *or* Micah 7. 8–end John 19. 17–30	G	Judith ch. 11 *or* Lev. 23. 1–22 2 Tim. 4. 9–end	Tobit ch. 10 *or* Micah 7. 8–end John 19. 17–30
Ps. 119. 33–56 Tobit ch. 11 *or* Hab. 1. 1–11 John 19. 31–end	G	Judith ch. 12 *or* Lev. 23. 23–end Titus ch. 1	Tobit ch. 11 *or* Hab. 1. 1–11 John 19. 31–end
Ps. 39; *40* Tobit ch. 12 *or* Hab. 1.12 – 2.5 John 20. 1–10	G	Judith ch. 13 *or* Lev. 24. 1–9 Titus ch. 2	Tobit ch. 12 *or* Hab. 1.12 – 2.5 John 20. 1–10
Ps. 35 Tobit 13.1 – 14.1 *or* Hab. 2. 6–end John 20. 11–18	G	Judith 15. 1–13 *or* Lev. 25. 1–24 Titus ch. 3	Tobit 13.1 – 14.1 *or* Hab. 2. 6–end John 20. 11–18
Ps. 45; *46* Tobit 14. 2–end *or* Hab. 3. 2–19a John 20. 19–end ct	**Crispin, Martyr at Rome, c. 287** Com. Martyr Gr	Judith 15.14 – 16.end *or* Num. 6. 1–5, 21–end Philemon	Tobit 14. 2–end *or* Hab. 3. 2–19a John 20. 19–end ct

October 2008

			Sunday Principal Service / Weekday Eucharist	Third Service / Morning Prayer
26	S	THE LAST SUNDAY AFTER TRINITY **(Proper 25)***		
		Track 1	Track 2	
		Deut. 34. 1–12	Lev. 19. 1–2, 15–18	Ps. 119. 137–152
		Ps. 90. 1–6 [13–17]	Ps. 1	Isa. 59. 9–20
		1 Thess. 2. 1–8	1 Thess. 2. 1–8	Luke 14. 1–14
	G	Matt. 22. 34–end	Matt. 22. 34–end	
		or, if being observed as Bible Sunday:		
			Neh. 8. 1–4a [5–6] 8–12	Ps. 119. 137–152
			Ps. 119. 9–16	Deut. 17. 14–15, 18–end
			Col. 3. 12–17	John 5. 36b–end
	G		Matt. 24. 30–35	
27 DEL 30	M		Eph. 4.32 – 5.8	Ps. 44
			Ps. 1	Gen. 18. 1–15
			Luke 13. 10–17	Matt. 27. 11–26
	G			
28	Tu	SIMON AND JUDE, APOSTLES		
			Isa. 28. 14–16	MP: Ps. 116; 117
			Ps. 119. 89–96	Wisd. 5. 1–16
			Eph. 2. 19–end	or Isa. 45. 18–end
	R		John 15. 17–end	Luke 6. 12–16
29	W	James Hannington, Bishop of Eastern Equatorial Africa, Martyr in Uganda, 1885		
		Com. Martyr *or*	Eph. 6. 1–9	Ps. 119. 57–80
		esp. Matt. 10. 28–39	Ps. 145. 10–20	Gen. 19. 1–3, 12–29
	Gr		Luke 13. 22–30	Matt. 27. 45–56
30	Th		Eph. 6. 10–20	Ps. 56; **57**; (63†)
			Ps. 144. 1–2, 9–11	Gen. 21. 1–21
	G		Luke 13. 31–end	Matt. 27. 57–end
31	F	Martin Luther, Reformer, 1546	Phil. 1. 1–11	Ps. **51**; 54
			Ps. 111	Gen. 22. 1–19
			Luke 14. 1–6	Matt. 28. 1–15
	G			

November 2008

1	Sa	**ALL SAINTS' DAY**	Rev. 7. 9–end	MP: Ps. 15; 84; 149
			Ps. 34. 1–10	Isa. ch. 35
			1 John 3. 1–3	Luke 9. 18–27
	W		Matt. 5. 1–12	
			Isa. 56. 3–8	MP: Ps. 111; 112; 117
		or, if the readings above are used on	*or* 2 Esdras 2. 42–end	Wisd. 5. 1–16
		Sunday 2 November:	Ps. 33. 1–5	*or* Jer. 31. 31–34
			Heb. 12. 18–24	2 Cor. 4. 5–12
	W		Matt. 5. 1–12	
		or, if kept as a feria:	Phil. 1. 18–26	Ps. 68
			Ps. 42. 1–7	Gen. ch. 23
			Luke 14. 1, 7–11	Matt. 28. 16–end
	G			

*If the Dedication Festival is kept on this Sunday, use the provision given on 4 and 5 October.

Second Service Evening Prayer	Calendar and Holy Communion	Morning Prayer	Evening Prayer
	THE TWENTY-THIRD SUNDAY AFTER TRINITY		
Ps. 119. 89–104 Eccles. chs 11 – 12 2 Tim. 2. 1–7 Gospel: Mark 12. 28–34 Ps. 119. 89–104 Isa. 55. 1–11 Luke 4. 14–30	Isa. 11. 1–10 Ps. 44. 1–9 Phil. 3. 17–end Matt. 22. 15–22 G	Ps. 119. 137–152 Isa. 59. 9–20 Luke 14. 11–24	Ps. 119. 89–104 Eccles. chs 11 – 12 2 Tim. 2. 1–7
Ps. **47**; 49 Hos. ch. 9 1 Cor. 12. 12–end *or First EP of Simon and Jude* Ps. 124; 125; 126 Deut. 32. 1–4 John 14. 15–26 **R** ct	G	Gen. 18. 1–15 Matt. 27. 11–26	Hos. ch. 9 1 Cor. 12. 12–end *or First EP of Simon and Jude* (Ps. 124; 125; 126) Deut. 32. 1–4 John 14. 15–26 **R** ct
	SIMON AND JUDE, APOSTLES		
EP: Ps. 119. 1–16 1 Macc. 2. 42–66 *or* Jer. 3. 11–18 Jude 1–4, 17–end	Isa. 28. 9–16 Ps. 116. 11–end Jude 1–8 *or* Rev. 21. 9–14 John 15. 17–end **R**	(Ps. 119. 89–96) Wisd. 5. 1–16 *or* Isa. 45. 18–end Luke 6. 12–16	(Ps. 119. 1–16) 1 Macc. 2. 42–66 *or* Jer. 3. 11–18 Eph. 2. 19–end
Ps. **59**; 60; (67) Hos. 11. 1–11 1 Cor. 14. 1–19	G	Gen. 19. 1–3, 12–29 Matt. 27. 45–56	Hos. 11. 1–11 1 Cor. 14. 1–19
Ps. 61; **62**; 64 Hos. 11.12 – 12.end 1 Cor. 14. 20–end	G	Gen. 21. 1–21 Matt. 27. 57–end	Hos. 11.12 – 12.end 1 Cor. 14. 20–end
First EP of All Saints Ps. 1; 5 Ecclus. 44. 1–15 *or* Isa. 40. 27–end Rev. 19. 6–10 W ct *or, if All Saints is observed on 2nd:* Ps. 38 Hos. 13. 1–14 1 Cor. 16. 1–9	G	Gen. 22. 1–19 Matt. 28. 1–15	*First EP of All Saints* Ps. 1; 5 Ecclus. 44. 1–15 *or* Isa. 40. 27–end Rev. 19. 6–10 W ct
	ALL SAINTS' DAY		
EP: Ps. 148; 150 Isa. 65. 17–end Heb. 11.32 – 12.2 EP: Ps. 145 Isa. 66. 20–23 Col. 1. 9–14 ct Ps. 65; **66** Hos. ch. 14 1 Cor. 16. 10–end ct	Isa. 66. 20–23 Ps. 33. 1–5 Rev. 7. 2–4 [5–8] 9–12 Matt. 5. 1–12 W	Ps. 15; 84; 149 Isa. ch. 35 Luke 9. 18–27	Ps. 148; 150 Isa. 65. 17–end Heb. 11.32 – 12.2

November 2008

			Sunday Principal Service / Weekday Eucharist	Third Service / Morning Prayer
2	S	THE FOURTH SUNDAY BEFORE ADVENT	Micah 3. 5–end Ps. 43 or Ps. 107. 1–8 I Thess. 2. 9–13	Ps. 33 Isa. 66. 20–23 Eph. 1. 11–end
	R or G		Matt. 24. 1–14	
	𝔚	Or ALL SAINTS' SUNDAY (see readings for 1 November throughout the day)		
3 DEL 31	M	**Commemoration of the Faithful Departed (All Souls' Day) (transferred from 2nd)** Lam. 3. 17–26, 31–33 or Wisd. 3. 1–9 Ps. 23 or Ps. 27. 1–15, 16–end Rom. 5. 5–11 or I Pet. 1. 3–9 John 5. 19–25 or John 6. 37–40		
	Rp or Gp	**Richard Hooker, Priest, Anglican Apologist, Teacher, 1600** Martin of Porres, Friar, 1639 Com. Teacher esp. John 16. 12–15 also Ecclus. 44. 10–15	or Phil. 2. 1–4 Ps. 131 Luke 14. 12–14	Ps. **2**; 146 alt. Ps. 71 Dan. ch. 1 Rev. ch. 1
	Rw or Gw			
4	Tu		Phil. 2. 5–11 Ps. 22. 22–27 Luke 14. 15–24	Ps. **5**; 147. 1–12 alt. Ps. 73 Dan. 2. 1–24 Rev. 2. 1–11
	R or G			
5	W		Phil. 2. 12–18 Ps. 27. 1–5 Luke 14. 25–33	Ps. **9**; 147. 13–end alt. Ps. 77 Dan. 2. 25–end Rev. 2. 12–end
	R or G			
6	Th	Leonard, Hermit, 6th century; William Temple, Archbishop of Canterbury, Teacher, 1944	Phil. 3. 3–8 Ps. 105. 1–7 Luke 15. 1–10	Ps. 11; **15**; 148 alt. Ps. 78. 1–39† Dan. 3. 1–18 Rev. 3. 1–13
	R or G			
7	F	**Willibrord of York, Bishop, Apostle of Frisia, 739** Com. Missionary esp. Isa. 52. 7–10 Matt. 28. 16–end	or Phil. 3.17 – 4.1 Ps. 122 Luke 16. 1–8	Ps. **16**; 149 alt. Ps. 55 Dan. 3. 19–end Rev. 3. 14–end
	Rw or Gw			
8	Sa	**The Saints and Martyrs of England** Isa. 61. 4–9 or Ecclus. 44. 1–15 Ps. 15 Rev. 19. 5–10 John 17. 18–23	or Phil. 4. 10–19 Ps. 112 Luke 16. 9–15	Ps. **18. 31–end**; 150 alt. Ps. **76**; 79 Dan. 4. 1–18 Rev. ch. 4
	Rw or Gw			
9	S	THE THIRD SUNDAY BEFORE ADVENT (Remembrance Sunday) Wisd. 6. 12–16 Canticle: Wisd. 6. 17–20 I Thess. 4. 13–end Matt. 25. 1–13	or Amos 5. 18–24 Ps. 70 I Thess. 4. 13–end Matt. 25. 1–13	Ps. 91 Deut. 17. 14–end I Tim. 2. 1–7
	R or G			
10 DEL 32	M	**Leo the Great, Bishop of Rome, Teacher, 461** Com. Teacher also I Pet. 5. 1–11	or Titus 1. 1–9 Ps. 24. 1–6 Luke 17. 1–6	Ps. 19; **20** alt. Ps. **80**; 82 Dan. 4. 19–end Rev. ch. 5
	Rw or Gw			
11	Tu	**Martin, Bishop of Tours, c. 397** Com. Bishop also I Thess. 5. 1–11 Matt. 25. 34–40	or Titus 2. 1–8, 11–14 Ps. 37. 3–5, 30–32 Luke 17. 7–10	Ps. **21**; 24 alt. Ps. 87; **89. 1–18** Dan. 5. 1–12 Rev. ch. 6
	Gw or Rw			

BOOK OF COMMON PRAYER 83

Second Service Evening Prayer	Calendar and Holy Communion	Morning Prayer	Evening Prayer
Ps. 111; 117 Dan. 7. 1–18 Luke 6. 17–31	**THE TWENTY-FOURTH SUNDAY AFTER TRINITY** Isa. 55. 6–11 Ps. 85. 1–7 Col. 1. 3–12 Matt. 9. 18–26 G	Ps. 33 Isa. 66. 20–23 Eph. 1. 11–end	Ps. 111; 117 Dan. 7. 1–18 Luke 6. 17–31
Ps. *92*; 96; 97 *alt.* Ps. *72*; 75 Isa. 1. 1–20 Matt. 1. 18–end	G	Dan. ch. 1 Rev. ch. 1	Isa. 1. 1–20 Matt. 1. 18–end
Ps. 98; 99; *100* *alt.* Ps. 74 Isa. 1. 21–end Matt. 2. 1–15	G	Dan. 2. 1–24 Rev. 2. 1–11	Isa. 1. 21–end Matt. 2. 1–15
Ps. 111; *112*; 116 *alt.* Ps. 119. 81–104 Isa. 2. 1–11 Matt. 2. 16–end	G	Dan. 2. 25–end Rev. 2. 12–end	Isa. 2. 1–11 Matt. 2. 16–end
Ps. 118 *alt.* Ps. 78. 40–end† Isa. 2. 12–end Matt. ch. 3	**Leonard, Hermit, 6th century** Com. Abbot Gw	Dan. 3. 1–18 Rev. 3. 1–13	Isa. 2. 12–end Matt. ch. 3
Ps. 137; 138; *143* *alt.* Ps. 69 Isa. 3. 1–15 Matt. 4. 1–11	G	Dan. 3. 19–end Rev. 3. 14–end	Isa. 3. 1–15 Matt. 4. 1–11
Ps. 145 *alt.* Ps. 81; *84* Isa. 4.2 – 5.7 Matt. 4. 12–22 ct	G	Dan. 4. 1–18 Rev. ch. 4	Isa. 4.2 – 5.7 Matt. 4. 12–22 ct
Ps. [20]; 82 Judges 7. 2–22 John 15. 9–17	**THE TWENTY-FIFTH SUNDAY AFTER TRINITY** 1 Sam. 10. 17–24 Ps. 97 Rom. 13. 1–7 Matt. 8. 23–34 G	Ps. 91 Deut. 17. 14–end 1 Tim. 2. 1–7	Ps. [20]; 82 Judges 7. 2–22 John 15. 9–17
Ps. 34 *alt.* Ps. *85*; 86 Isa. 5. 8–24 Matt. 4.23 – 5.12	G	Dan. 4. 19–end Rev. ch. 5	Isa. 5. 8–24 Matt. 4.23 – 5.12
Ps. 36; *40* *alt.* Ps. 89. 19–end Isa. 5. 25–end Matt. 5. 13–20	**Martin, Bishop of Tours, *c.* 397** Com. Bishop Gw	Dan. 5. 1–12 Rev. ch. 6	Isa. 5. 25–end Matt. 5. 13–20

84 COMMON WORSHIP

November 2008

		Sunday Principal Service Weekday Eucharist	Third Service Morning Prayer
12	W R or G	Titus 3. 1–7 Ps. 23 Luke 17. 11–19	Ps. **23**; 25 alt. Ps. 119. 105–128 Dan. 5. 13–end Rev. 7. 1–4, 9–end
13	Th Rw or Gw	**Charles Simeon, Priest, Evangelical Divine, 1836** Com. Pastor or Philemon 7–20 esp. Mal. 2. 5–7 Ps. 146. 4–end also Col. 1. 3–8 Luke 17. 20–25 Luke 8. 4–8	Ps. **26**; 27 alt. Ps. 90; **92** Dan. ch. 6 Rev. ch. 8
14	F R or G	**Samuel Seabury, first Anglican Bishop in North America, 1796** 2 John 4–9 Ps. 119. 1–8 Luke 17. 26–end	Ps. 28; **32** alt. Ps. **88**; (95) Dan. 7. 1–14 Rev. 9. 1–12
15	Sa R or G	3 John 5–8 Ps. 112 Luke 18. 1–8	Ps. 33 alt. 96; **97**; 100 Dan. 7. 15–end Rev. 9. 13–end
16	S Rw or Gw	**THE SECOND SUNDAY BEFORE ADVENT** Zeph. 1. 7, 12–end Ps. 90. 1–8 [9–11] 12 1 Thess. 5. 1–11 Matt. 25. 14–30	Ps. 98 Dan. 10. 19–end Rev. ch. 4
17 DEL 33	M Rw or Gw	**Hugh, Bishop of Lincoln, 1200** Com. Bishop or Rev. 1. 1–4; 2. 1–5 also 1 Tim. 6. 11–16 Ps. 1 Luke 18. 35–end	Ps.46; **47** alt. Ps. **98**; 99; 101 Dan. 8. 1–14 Rev. ch. 10
18	Tu Rw or Gw	**Elizabeth of Hungary, Princess of Thuringia, Philanthropist, 1231** Com. Saint or Rev. 3. 1–6, 14–end esp. Matt. 25. 31–end Ps. 15 also Prov. 31. 10–end Luke 19. 1–10	Ps. 48; **52** Ps. **106**† (or 103) Dan. 8. 15–end Rev. 11. 1–14
19	W Rw or Gw	**Hilda, Abbess of Whitby, 680** **Mechtild, Beguine of Magdeburg, Mystic, 1280** Com. Religious or Rev. ch. 4 esp. Isa. 61.10 – 62.5 Ps. 150 Luke 19. 11–28	Ps. **56**; 57 Ps. 110; **111**; 112 Dan. 9. 1–19 Rev. 11. 15–end
20	Th R or Gr	**Edmund, King of the East Angles, Martyr, 870** **Priscilla Lydia Sellon, a Restorer of the Religious Life in the Church of England, 1876** Com. Martyr or Rev. 5. 1–10 also Prov. 20. 28; 21. 1–4, 7 Ps. 149. 1–5 Luke 19. 41–44	Ps. 61; **62** alt. Ps. 113; **115** Dan. 9. 20–end Rev. ch. 12
21	F R or G	Rev. 10. 8–11 Ps. 119. 65–72 Luke 19. 45–end	Ps. **63**; 65 alt. Ps. 139 Dan. 10.1 – 11.1 Rev. 13. 1–10
22	Sa R or G	**Cecilia, Martyr at Rome, c. 230** Rev. 11. 4–12 Ps. 144. 1–9 Luke 20. 27–40	Ps. 78. 1–39 alt. Ps. 120; **121**; 122 Dan. ch. 12 Rev. 13. 11–end

BOOK OF COMMON PRAYER

Second Service Evening Prayer		Calendar and Holy Communion	Morning Prayer	Evening Prayer
Ps. 37 *alt*. Ps. *91*; 93 Isa. ch. 6 Matt. 5. 21–37	G		Dan. 5. 13–end Rev. 7. 1–4, 9–end	Isa. ch. 6 Matt. 5. 21–37
Ps. 42; *43* *alt*. Ps. 94 Isa. 7. 1–17 Matt. 5. 38–end	Gw	**Britius, Bishop of Tours, 444** Com. Bishop	Dan. ch. 6 Rev. ch. 8	Isa. 7. 1–17 Matt. 5. 38–end
Ps. 31 *alt*. Ps. 102 Isa. 8. 1–15 Matt. 6. 1–18	G		Dan. 7. 1–14 Rev. 9. 1–12	Isa. 8. 1–15 Matt. 6. 1–18
Ps. 84; *86* *alt*. Ps. 104 Isa. 8.16 – 9.7 Matt. 6. 19–end ct	Gw	**Machutus, Bishop, Apostle of Brittany, c. 564** Com. Bishop	Dan. 7. 15–end Rev. 9. 13–end	Isa. 8.16 – 9.7 Matt. 6. 19–end ct
Ps. 89. 19–29 [30–37] 1 Kings 1. [1–14] 15–40 Rev. 1. 4–18 *Gospel*: Luke 9. 1–6	G	**THE TWENTY-SIXTH SUNDAY AFTER TRINITY** Hos. 6. 4–6 Ps. 118. 14–21 Col. 3. 12–17 Matt. 13. 24b–30	Ps. 98 Dan. 10. 19–end Rev. ch. 4	Ps. 89. 19–29 [30–37] 1 Kings 1. [1–14] 15–40 Rev. 1. 4–18
Ps. 70; *71* *alt*. Ps. *105*† (or 103) Isa. 9.8 – 10.4 Matt. 7. 1–12	Gw	**Hugh, Bishop of Lincoln, 1200** Com. Bishop	Dan. 8. 1–14 Rev. ch. 10	Isa. 9.8 – 10.4 Matt. 7. 1–12
Ps. *67*; 72 *alt*. Ps. 107† Isa. 10. 5–19 Matt. 7. 13–end	G		Dan. 8. 15–end Rev. 11. 1–14	Isa. 10. 5–19 Matt. 7. 13–end
Ps. 73 *alt*. Ps. 119. 129–152 Isa. 10. 20–32 Matt. 8. 1–13	G		Dan. 9. 1–19 Rev. 11. 15–end	Isa. 10. 20–32 Matt. 8. 1–13
Ps. 74; *76* *alt*. Ps. 114; *116*; 117 Isa. 10.33 – 11.9 Matt. 8. 14–22	Gr	**Edmund, King of the East Angles, Martyr, 870** Com. Martyr	Dan. 9. 20–end Rev. ch. 12	Isa. 10.33 – 11.9 Matt. 8. 14–22
Ps. 77 *alt*. Ps. *130*; 131; 137 Isa. 11.10 – 12.end Matt. 8. 23–end	G		Dan. 10.1 – 11.1 Rev. 13. 1–10	Isa. 11.10 – 12.end Matt. 8. 23–end
Ps. 78. 40–end *alt*. Ps. 118 Isa. 13. 1–13 Matt. 9. 1–17 ct *or First EP of Christ the King* Ps. 99; 100 Isa. 10.33 – 11.9 1 Tim. 6. 11–16 **R** *or* **W** ct	Gr	**Cecilia, Martyr at Rome, c. 230** Com. Virgin Martyr	Dan. ch. 12 Rev. 13. 11–end	Isa. 13. 1–13 Matt. 9. 1–17 ct

COMMON WORSHIP

November 2008

			Sunday Principal Service / Weekday Eucharist	Third Service / Morning Prayer
23	S	**CHRIST THE KING** The Sunday Next Before Advent		
			Ezek. 34. 11–16, 20–24	MP: Ps. 29; 110
			Ps. 95. 1–7	Isa. 4.2 – 5.7
			Eph. 1. 15–end	Luke 19. 29–38
	R or W		Matt. 25. 31–end	
24 DEL 34	M		Rev. 14. 1–5	Ps. 92; **96**
			Ps. 24. 1–6	alt. Ps. 123; 124; 125; **126**
			Luke 21. 1–4	Isa. 40. 1–11
	R or G			Rev. 14. 1–13
25	Tu	Catherine of Alexandria, Martyr, 4th century; Isaac Watts, Hymn Writer, 1748		
			Rev. 14. 14–19	Ps. **97**; 98; 100
			Ps. 96	alt. Ps. **132**; 133
			Luke 21. 5–11	Isa. 40. 12–26
	R or G			Rev. 14.14 – 15.end
26	W		Rev. 15. 1–4	Ps. 110; 111; **112**
			Ps. 98	alt. Ps. 119. 153–end
			Luke 21. 12–19	Isa. 40.27 – 41.7
	R or G			Rev. 16. 1–11
27	Th		Rev. 18. 1–2, 21–23; 19. 1–3, 9	Ps. **125**; 126; 127; 128
			Ps. 100	alt. Ps. **143**; 146
			Luke 21. 20–28	Isa. 41. 8–20
	R or G			Rev. 16. 12–end
28	F		Rev. 20.1–4, 11 – 21.2	Ps. 139
			Ps. 84. 1–6	alt. Ps. 142; **144**
			Luke 21. 29–33	Isa. 41.21 – 42.9
	R or G			Rev. ch. 17
29	Sa		Rev. 22. 1–7	Ps. 145
			Ps. 95. 1–7	alt. Ps. 147
			Luke 21. 34–36	Isa. 42. 10–17
				Rev. ch. 18
		Day of Intercession and Thanksgiving for the Missionary Work of the Church	Isa. 49. 1–6; Isa. 52. 7–10; Mic. 4. 1–5 Acts 17. 12–end; 2 Cor. 5.14 – 6.2; Eph. 2. 13–end Ps. 2; 46; 47	
	R or G		Matt. 5. 13–16; Matt. 28. 16–end; John 17. 20–end	
30	S	**THE FIRST SUNDAY OF ADVENT** (Andrew transferred to 1 Dec.) CW Year B begins		
			Isa. 64. 1–9	Ps. 44
			Ps. 80. 1–8 [18–20]	Isa. 2. 1–5
			1 Cor. 1. 3–9	Luke 12. 35–48
			Mark 13. 24–end	
	P			

December 2008

1	M	**ANDREW THE APOSTLE** (transferred from 30 Nov.)		
			Isa. 52. 7–10	MP: Ps. 47; 147. 1–12
			Ps. 19. 1–6	Ezek. 47. 1–12
			Rom. 10. 12–18	or Ecclus. 14. 20–end
	R		Matt. 4. 18–22	John 12. 20–32
2	Tu	Daily Eucharistic Lectionary Year 1 begins		
			Isa. 11. 1–10	Ps. **80**; 82
			Ps. 72. 1–4, 18–19	alt. Ps. **5**; 6; (8)
			Luke 10. 21–24	Isa. 43. 1–13
	P			Rev. ch. 20

Second Service Evening Prayer		Calendar and Holy Communion	Morning Prayer	Evening Prayer
		THE SUNDAY NEXT BEFORE ADVENT To celebrate Christ the King, see *Common Worship* provision.		
EP: Ps. 93; [97] 2 Sam. 23. 1–7 or 1 Macc. 2. 15–29 Matt. 28. 16–end	G	Jer. 23. 5–8 Ps. 85. 8–end Col. 1. 13–20 John 6. 5–14	Ps. 29; 110 Isa. 4.2 – 5.7 Luke 19. 29–38	Ps. 93; [97] 2 Sam. 23. 1–7 or 1 Macc. 2. 15–29 Matt. 28. 16–end
Ps. *80*; 81 alt. Ps. *127*; 128; 129 Isa. 14. 3–20 Matt. 9. 18–34	G		Isa. 40. 1–11 Rev. 14. 1–13	Isa. 14. 3–20 Matt. 9. 18–34
		Catherine of Alexandria, Martyr, 4th century		
Ps. 99; *101* alt. Ps. (134); *135* Isa. ch. 17 Matt. 9.35 – 10.15	Gr	Com. Virgin Martyr	Isa. 40. 12–26 Rev. 14.14 – 15.end	Isa. ch. 17 Matt. 9.35 – 10.15
Ps. 121; *122*; 123; 124 alt. Ps. 136 Isa. ch. 19 Matt. 10. 16–33	G		Isa. 40.27 – 41.7 Rev. 16. 1–11	Isa. ch. 19 Matt. 10. 16–33
Ps. 131; 132; *133* alt. Ps. *138*; 140; 141 Isa. 21. 1–12 Matt. 10.34 – 11.1	G		Isa. 41. 8–20 Rev. 16. 12–end	Isa. 21. 1–12 Matt. 10.34 – 11.1
Ps. *146*; 147 alt. Ps. 145 Isa. 22. 1–14 Matt. 11. 2–19	G		Isa. 41.21 – 42.9 Rev. ch. 17	Isa. 22. 1–14 Matt. 11. 2–19
Ps. 148; 149; *150* alt. Ps. *148*; 149; 150 Isa. ch. 24 Matt. 11. 20–end **P ct**	G		Isa. 42. 10–17 Rev. ch. 18	Isa. ch. 24 Matt. 11. 20–end **P ct**
	G	To celebrate the Day of Intercession and Thanksgiving for the Missionary Work of the Church, see *Common Worship* provision.		
		THE FIRST SUNDAY IN ADVENT (Andrew transferred to 1 Dec.) Advent 1 Collect until Christmas Eve		
Ps. 25. 1–9 [10–end] Isa. 1. 1–20 Matt. 21. 1–13 or First EP of Andrew the Apostle Ps. 48 Isa. 49. 1–9a 1 Cor. 4. 9–16 **R ct**	P	Mic. 4. 1–4, 6–7 Ps. 25. 1–9 Rom. 13. 8–14 Matt. 21. 1–13	Ps. 44 Isa. 2. 1–5 Luke 12. 35–48	Ps. 9 Isa. 1. 1–20 Mark 13. 24–37 or First EP of Andrew the Apostle Ps. 48 Isa. 49. 1–9a 1 Cor. 4. 9–16 **R ct**
		ANDREW THE APOSTLE (transferred from 30 Nov.)		
EP: Ps. 87; 96 Zech. 8. 20–end John 1. 35–42	R	Zech. 8. 20–end Ps. 92. 1–5 Rom. 10. 9–end Matt. 4. 18–22	(Ps. 47; 147. 1–12) Ezek. 47. 1–12 or Ecclus. 14. 20–end John 12. 20–32	(Ps. 87; 96) Isa. 52. 7–10 John 1. 35–42
Ps. *74*; 75 alt. Ps. *9*; 10† Isa. 26. 1–13 Matt. 12. 22–37	P		Isa. 43. 1–13 Rev. ch. 20	Isa. 26. 1–13 Matt. 12. 22–37

December 2008

			Sunday Principal Service Weekday Eucharist	Third Service Morning Prayer
3	W P	Francis Xavier, Missionary, Apostle of the Indies, 1552	Isa. 25. 6–10a Ps. 23 Matt. 15. 29–37	Ps. 5; *7* *alt.* Ps. 119. 1–32 Isa. 43. 14–end Rev. 21. 1–8
4	Th P	John of Damascus, Monk, Teacher, c. 749; Nicholas Ferrar, Deacon, Founder of the Little Gidding Community, 1637	Isa. 26. 1–6 Ps. 118. 18–27a Matt. 7. 21, 24–27	Ps. *42*; 43 *alt.* Ps. 14; *15*; 16 Isa. 44. 1–8 Rev. 21. 9–21
5	F P		Isa. 29. 17–end Ps. 27. 1–4, 16–17 Matt. 9. 27–31	Ps. *25*; 26 *alt.* Ps. 17; *19* Isa. 44. 9–23 Rev. 21.22 – 22.5
6	Sa Pw	**Nicholas, Bishop of Myra, c. 326** Com. Bishop *or* *also* Isa. 61. 1–3 1 Tim. 6. 6–11 Mark 10. 13–16	Isa. 30. 19–21, 23–26 Ps. 146. 4–9 Matt. 9.35 – 10.1, 6–8	Ps. *9*; (10) *alt.* Ps. 20; 21; *23* Isa. 44.24 – 45.13 Rev. 22. 6–end
7	S P	THE SECOND SUNDAY OF ADVENT	Isa. 40. 1–11 Ps. 85. [1–2] 8–end 2 Pet. 3. 8–15a Mark 1. 1–8	Ps. 80 Baruch 5. 1–9 *or* Zeph. 3. 14–end Luke 1. 5–20
8	M Pw	**The Conception of the Blessed Virgin Mary** Com. BVM *or*	Isa. ch. 35 Ps. 85. 7–end Luke 5. 17–26	Ps. 44 *alt.* Ps. 27; *30* Isa. 45. 14–end 1 Thess. ch. 1
9	Tu P		Isa. 40. 1–11 Ps. 96. 1, 10–end Matt. 18. 12–14	Ps. *56*; 57 *alt.* Ps. 32; *36* Isa. ch. 46 1 Thess. 2. 1–12
10	W P	Ember Day*	Isa. 40. 25–end Ps. 103. 8–13 Matt. 11. 28–end	Ps. *62*; 63 *alt.* Ps. 34 Isa. ch. 47 1 Thess. 2. 13–end
11	Th P		Isa. 41. 13–20 Ps. 145. 1, 8–13 Matt. 11. 11–15	Ps. 53; *54*; 60 *alt.* Ps. 37† Isa. 48. 1–11 1 Thess. ch. 3
12	F P	Ember Day*	Isa. 48. 17–19 Ps. 1 Matt. 11. 16–19	Ps. 85; *86* *alt.* Ps. 31 Isa. 48. 12–end 1 Thess. 4. 1–12
13	Sa Pr	**Lucy, Martyr at Syracuse, 304** Ember Day* Samuel Johnson, Moralist, 1784 Com. Martyr *or* *also* Wisd. 3. 1–7 2 Cor. 4. 6–15	Ecclus. 48. 1–4, 9–11 *or* 2 Kings 2. 9–12 Ps. 80. 1–4, 18–19 Matt. 17. 10–13	Ps. 145 *alt.* Ps. 41; *42*; 43 Isa. 49. 1–13 1 Thess. 4. 13–end

*For Ember Day provision, see p. 13.

BOOK OF COMMON PRAYER

Second Service Evening Prayer	Calendar and Holy Communion	Morning Prayer	Evening Prayer
Ps. 76; **77** *alt.* Ps. **11**; 12; 13 Isa. 28. 1–13 Matt. 12. 38–end	P	Isa. 43. 14–end Rev. 21. 1–8	Isa. 28. 1–13 Matt. 12. 38–end
Ps. **40**; 46 *alt.* Ps. 18† Isa. 28. 14–end Matt. 13. 1–23	P	Isa. 44. 1–8 Rev. 21. 9–21	Isa. 28. 14–end Matt. 13. 1–23
Ps. 16; **17** *alt.* Ps. 22 Isa. 29. 1–14 Matt. 13. 24–43	P	Isa. 44. 9–23 Rev. 21.22 – 22.5	Isa. 29. 1–14 Matt. 13. 24–43
Ps. **27**; 28 *alt.* Ps. **24**; 25 Isa. 29. 15–end Matt. 13. 44–end ct	**Nicholas, Bishop of Myra, c. 326** Com. Bishop Pw	Isa. 44.24–45.13 Rev. 22. 6–end	Isa. 29. 15–end Matt. 13. 44–end ct
Ps. 40. [1–11] 12–end 1 Kings 22. 1–28 Rom. 15. 4–13 *Gospel:* Matt. 11. 2–11	**THE SECOND SUNDAY IN ADVENT** 2 Kings 22. 8–10; 23. 1–3 Ps. 50. 1–6 Rom. 15. 4–13 Luke 21. 25–33 P	Ps. 80 Baruch 5. 1–9 *or* Zeph. 3. 14–end Luke 1. 5–20	Ps. 40. [1–11] 12–end 1 Kings 22. 1–28 2 Pet. 3. 8–15a
Ps. **144**; 146 *alt.* Ps. 26; **28**; 29 Isa. 30. 1–18 Matt. 14. 1–12	**The Conception of the Blessed Virgin Mary** Pw	Isa. 45. 14–end 1 Thess. ch. 1	Isa. 30. 1–18 Matt. 14. 1–12
Ps. **11**; 12; 13 *alt.* Ps. 33 Isa. 30. 19–end Matt. 14. 13–end	P	Isa. ch. 46 1 Thess. 2. 1–12	Isa. 30. 19–end Matt. 14. 13–end
Ps. **10**; 14 *alt.* Ps. 119. 33–56 Isa. ch. 31 Matt. 15. 1–20	P	Isa. ch. 47 1 Thess. 2. 13–end	Isa. ch. 31 Matt. 15. 1–20
Ps. 73 *alt.* Ps. 39; **40** Isa. ch. 32 Matt. 15. 21–28	P	Isa. 48. 1–11 1 Thess. ch. 3	Isa. ch. 32 Matt. 15. 21–28
Ps. 82; **90** *alt.* Ps. 35 Isa. 33. 1–22 Matt. 15. 29–end	P	Isa. 48. 12–end 1 Thess. 4. 1–12	Isa. 33. 1–22 Matt. 15. 29–end
	Lucy, Martyr at Syracuse, 304 Com. Virgin Martyr		
Ps. 93; **94** *alt.* Ps. 45; **46** Isa. ch. 35 Matt. 16. 1–12 ct	Pr	Isa. 49. 1–13 1 Thess. 4. 13–end	Isa. ch. 35 Matt. 16. 1–12 ct

December 2008

			Sunday Principal Service / Weekday Eucharist	Third Service / Morning Prayer
14	S	THE THIRD SUNDAY OF ADVENT	Isa. 61. 1–4, 8–end Ps. 126 or Canticle: Magnificat 1 Thess. 5. 16–24 John 1. 6–8, 19–28	Ps. 50. 1–6, 62 Isa. ch. 12 Luke 1. 57–66
	Pw			
15	M		Num. 24. 2–7, 15–17 Ps. 25. 3–8 Matt. 21. 23–27	Ps. 40 *alt.* Ps. 44 Isa. 49. 14–25 1 Thess. 5. 1–11
	P			
16	Tu		Zeph. 3. 1–2, 9–13 Ps. 34. 1–6, 21–22 Matt. 21. 28–32	Ps. *70*; 74 *alt.* Ps. *48*; 52 Isa. ch. 50 1 Thess. 5. 12–end
	P			
17	W	O Sapientia Eglantyne Jebb, Social Reformer, Founder of 'Save the Children', 1928	Gen. 49. 2, 8–10 Ps. 72. 1–5, 18–19 Matt. 1. 1–17	Ps. *75*; 96 *alt.* Ps. 119. 57–80 Isa. 51. 1–8 2 Thess. ch. 1
	P			
18	Th		Jer. 23. 5–8 Ps. 72. 1–2, 12–13, 18–end Matt. 1. 18–24	Ps. *76*; 97 *alt.* Ps. 56; *57*; (63†) Isa. 51. 9–16 2 Thess. ch. 2
	P			
19	F		Judg. 13. 2–7, 24–end Ps. 71. 3–8 Luke 1. 5–25	Ps. 144; *146* Isa. 51. 17–end 2 Thess. ch. 3
	P			
20	Sa		Isa. 7. 10–14 Ps. 24. 1–6 Luke 1. 26–38	Ps. *46*; 95 Isa. 52. 1–12 Jude
	P			
21	S	THE FOURTH SUNDAY OF ADVENT	2 Sam. 7. 1–11, 16 Canticle: Magnificat or Ps. 89. 1–4, 19–26 (or 1–8) Rom. 16. 25–end Luke 1. 26–38	Ps. 144 Isa. 7. 10–16 Rom. 1. 1–7
	P			
22	M*		1 Sam. 1. 24–end Ps. 113 Luke 1. 46–56	Ps. *124*; 125; 126; 127 Isa. 52.13 – 53.end 2 Pet. 1. 1–15
	P			
23	Tu		Mal. 3. 1–4; 4. 5–end Ps. 25. 3–9 Luke 1. 57–66	Ps. 128; 129; *130*; 131 Isa. ch. 54 2 Pet. 1.16 – 2.3
	P			
24	W	CHRISTMAS EVE	*Morning Eucharist* 2 Sam. 7. 1–5, 8–11, 16 Ps. 89. 2, 19–27 Acts 13. 16–26 Luke 1. 67–79	Ps. *45*; 113 Isa. ch. 55 2 Pet. 2. 4–end
	P			

*Thomas the Apostle may be celebrated on 22 December (transferred from 21st) instead of 3 July.

BOOK OF COMMON PRAYER

Second Service Evening Prayer	Calendar and Holy Communion	Morning Prayer	Evening Prayer
Ps. 68. 1–8 [9–19] Mal. 3. 1–4; ch. 4 Phil. 4. 4–7 *Gospel*: Matt. 14. 1–12	**THE THIRD SUNDAY IN ADVENT** Isa. ch. 35 Ps. 80. 1–7 1 Cor. 4. 1–5 Matt. 11. 2–10 **P**	Ps. 62 Isa. ch. 12 Luke 1. 57–66	Ps. 68. 1–8 [9–19] Mal. 3. 1–4; ch. 4 Matt. 14. 1–12
Ps. 25; **26** *alt.* Ps. **47**; 49 Isa. 38. 1–8, 21–22 Matt. 16. 13–end	**P**	Isa. 49. 14–25 1 Thess. 5. 1–11	Isa. 38. 1–8, 21–22 Matt. 16. 13–end
Ps. **50**; 54 *alt.* Ps. 50 Isa. 38. 9–20 Matt. 17. 1–13	O Sapientia **P**	Isa. ch. 50 1 Thess. 5. 12–end	Isa. 38. 9–20 Matt. 17. 1–13
Ps. 25; **82** *alt.* Ps. **59**; 60; (67) Isa. ch. 39 Matt. 17. 14–21	Ember Day Ember CEG **P**	Isa. 51. 1–8 2 Thess. ch. 1	Isa. ch. 39 Matt. 17. 14–21
Ps. 44 *alt.* Ps. 61; **62**; 64 Zeph. 1.1 – 2.3 Matt. 17. 22–end	**P**	Isa. 51. 9–16 2 Thess. ch. 2	Zeph. 1.1 – 2.3 Matt. 17. 22–end
Ps. 10; **57** Zeph. 3. 1–13 Matt. 18. 1–20	Ember Day Ember CEG **P**	Isa. 51. 17–end 2 Thess. ch. 3	Zeph. 3. 1–13 Matt. 18. 1–20
Ps. **4**; 9 Zeph. 3. 14–end Matt. 18. 21–end ct	Ember Day Ember CEG **P**	Isa. 52. 1–12 Jude	Zeph. 3. 14–end Matt. 18. 21–end ct
Ps. 113; [131] Zech. 2. 10–end Luke 1. 39–55	**THE FOURTH SUNDAY IN ADVENT** Isa. 40. 1–9 Ps. 145. 17–end Phil. 4. 4–7 John 1. 19–28 **P**	Ps. 144 Isa. 7. 10–16 Rom. 1. 1–7	Ps. 113; [131] Zech. 2. 10–end Luke 1. 39–55 or First EP of Thomas (Ps. 27) Isa. ch. 35 Heb. 10.35 – 11.1 **R** ct
Ps. 24; **48** Mal. 1. 1, 6–end Matt. 19. 1–12	**THOMAS THE APOSTLE** (transferred from 21st) Job 42. 1–6 Ps. 139. 1–11 Eph. 2. 19–end John 20. 24–end **R**	(Ps. 92; 146) 2 Sam. 15. 17–21 or Ecclus. ch. 2 John 11. 1–16	(Ps. 139) Hab. 2. 1–4 1 Pet. 1. 3–12
Ps. 89. 1–37 Mal. 2. 1–16 Matt. 19. 13–15	**P**	Isa. ch. 54 2 Pet. 1.16 – 2.3	Mal. 2. 1–16 Matt. 19. 13–15
Ps. 85 Zech. ch. 2 Rev. 1. 1–8	**CHRISTMAS EVE** Coll. (1) Christmas Eve (2) Advent 1 Mic. 5. 2–5a Ps. 24 Titus 3. 3–7 Luke 2. 1–14 **P**	Isa. ch. 55 2 Pet. 2. 4–end	Ps. 85 Zech. ch. 2 Rev. 1. 1–8

December 2008

			Sunday Principal Service / Weekday Eucharist	Third Service / Morning Prayer

25 Th **CHRISTMAS DAY**
Any of the following sets of readings may be used on the evening of Christmas Eve and on Christmas Day. Set III should be used at some service during the celebration.

I
Isa. 9. 2–7
Ps. 96
Titus 2. 11–14
Luke 2. 1–14 [15–20]
II
Isa. 62. 6–end
Ps. 97
Titus 3. 4–7
Luke 2. [1–7] 8–20
III
Isa. 52. 7–10
Ps. 98
Heb. 1. 1–4 [5–12]
John 1. 1–14

MP: Ps. *110*; 117
Isa. 62. 1–5
Matt. 1. 18–end

W

26 F **STEPHEN, DEACON, FIRST MARTYR**
The reading from Acts must be used as either the first or second reading at the Eucharist.

2 Chron. 24. 20–22
or Acts 7. 51–end
Ps. 119. 161–168
Acts 7. 51–end
or Gal. 2. 16b–20
Matt. 10. 17–22

MP: Ps. *13*; 31. 1–8; 150
Jer. 26. 12–15
Acts ch. 6

R

27 Sa **JOHN, APOSTLE AND EVANGELIST**

Exod. 33. 7–11a
Ps. 117
1 John ch. 1
John 21. 19b–end

MP: Ps. *21*; 147. 13–end
Exod. 33. 12–end
1 John 2. 1–11

W

28 S **THE HOLY INNOCENTS**

Jer. 31. 15–17
Ps. 124
1 Cor. 1. 26–29
Matt. 2. 13–18

MP: Ps. *36*; 146
Baruch 4. 21–27
or Gen. 37. 13–20
Matt. 18. 1–10

R

or, for The First Sunday of Christmas:

Isa. 61.10 – 62.3
Ps. 148. 1–6 [7–end]
Gal. 4. 4–7
Luke 2. 15–21

Ps. 105. 1–11
Isa. 63. 7–9
Eph. 3. 5–12

W

29 M **Thomas Becket, Archbishop of Canterbury, Martyr, 1170***
For Holy Innocents, see 28th.
Com. Martyr
  esp. Matt. 10. 28–33
  also Ecclus. 51. 1–8
or
1 John 2. 3–11
Ps. 96. 1–4
Luke 2. 22–35

Ps. *19*; 20
Isa. 57. 15–end
John 1. 1–18

Wr

30 Tu

1 John 2. 12–17
Ps. 96. 7–10
Luke 2. 36–40

Ps. 111; 112; *113*
Isa. 59. 1–15a
John 1. 19–28

W

31 W *John Wyclif, Reformer, 1384*

1 John 2. 18–21
Ps. 96. 1, 11–end
John 1. 1–18

Ps. 102
Isa. 59. 15b–end
John 1. 29–34

W

---

*Thomas Becket may be celebrated on 7 July instead of 29 December.

Second Service Evening Prayer	Calendar and Holy Communion	Morning Prayer	Evening Prayer
EP: Ps. 8 Isa. 65. 17–25 Phil. 2. 5–11 or Luke 2. 1–20 *if it has not been used at the principal service of the day*	**CHRISTMAS DAY** Isa. 9. 2–7 Ps. 98 Heb. 1. 1–12 John 1. 1–14	Ps. 110; 117 Isa. 62. 1–5 Matt. 1. 18–end	Ps. 8 Isa. 65. 17–25 Phil. 2. 5–11 or Luke 2. 1–20
	W		
EP: Ps. 57; **86** Gen. 4. 1–10 Matt. 23. 34–end	**STEPHEN, DEACON, FIRST MARTYR** Collect (1) Stephen (2) Christmas 2 Chron. 24. 20–22 Ps. 119. 161–168 Acts 7. 55–end R Matt. 23. 34–end	(Ps. 13; 31. 1–8; 150) Jer. 26. 12–15 Acts ch. 6	(Ps. 57; 86) Gen. 4. 1–10 Matt. 10. 17–22
EP: Ps. 97 Isa. 6. 1–8 1 John 5. 1–12	**JOHN, APOSTLE AND EVANGELIST** Collect (1) John (2) Christmas Exod. 33. 18–end Ps. 92. 11–end 1 John ch. 1 W John 21. 19b–end	(Ps. 21; 147. 13–end) Exod. 33. 7–11a 1 John 2. 1–11	(Ps. 97) Isa. 6. 1–8 1 John 5. 1–12
EP: Ps. 123; **128** Isa. 49. 14–25 Mark 10. 13–16	**THE HOLY INNOCENTS** Collect (1) Innocents (2) Christmas Jer. 31. 10–17 Ps. 123 Rev. 14. 1–5 R Matt. 2. 13–18	(Ps. 36; 146) Baruch 4. 21–27 or Gen. 37. 13–20 Matt. 18. 1–10	(Ps. 124; 128) Isa. 49. 14–25 Mark 10. 13–16
Ps. 132 Isa. ch. 35 Col. 1. 9–20 or Luke 2. 41–end	*or, for The First Sunday after Christmas Day* Isa. 62. 10–12 Ps. 45. 1–7 Gal. 4. 1–7 W Matt. 1. 18–end	Ps. 105. 1–11 Isa. 63. 7–9 Eph. 3. 5–12	Ps. 132 Isa. ch. 35 1 John 1. 1–7
Ps. 131; **132** Jonah ch. 1 Col. 1. 1–14	CEG of Christmas W	Isa. 57. 15–end John 1. 1–18	Jonah ch. 1 Col. 1. 1–14
Ps. **65**; 84 Jonah ch. 2 Col. 1. 15–23	W	Isa. 59. 1–15a John 1. 19–28	Jonah ch. 2 Col. 1. 15–23
Ps. **90**; 148 Jonah chs 3 – 4 Col. 1.24 – 2.7 or First EP of The Naming of Jesus Ps. 148 Jer. 23. 1–6 Col. 2. 8–15 ct	**Silvester, Bishop of Rome, 335** Com. Bishop W	Isa. 59. 15b–end John 1. 29–34	Jonah chs 3 – 4 Col. 1.24 – 2.7 or First EP of The Circumcision of Christ (Ps. 148) Jer. 23. 1–6 Col. 2. 8–15 ct

CALENDAR 2008

		JANUARY						FEBRUARY						MARCH			
Su	..	E	B	E^3	E^4	Su	..	L^{-1}	L^1	L^2	L^3	Su	..	L^4	L^5	P	E	E^2
M	..	7	14	21	28	M	..	4	11	18	25	M	..	3	10	17	24	An
Tu	1	8	15	22	29	Tu	..	5	12	19	26	Tu	..	4	11	18	25	..
W	2	9	16	23	30	W	..	A	13	20	27	W	..	5	12	19	26	..
Th	3	10	17	24	31	Th	..	7	14	21	28	Th	..	6	13	M	27	..
F	4	11	18	25	..	F	1	8	15	22	29	F	..	7	14	G	28	..
Sa	5	12	19	26	..	Sa	Pr	9	16	23	..	Sa	1	8	15	22	29	..

		APRIL						MAY						JUNE			
Su	..	E^3	E^4	E^5	E^6	Su	..	E^7	W	T	T^1	Su	T^2	T^3	T^4	T^5	T^6	..
M	..	7	14	21	28	M	..	5	12	19	26	M	2	9	16	23	30	..
Tu	1	8	15	22	29	Tu	..	6	13	20	27	Tu	3	10	17	24	..	..
W	2	9	16	23	30	W	..	7	14	21	28	W	4	11	18	25	..	..
Th	3	10	17	24	..	Th	A	8	15	22	29	Th	5	12	19	26	..	..
F	4	11	18	25	..	F	2	9	16	23	30	F	6	13	20	27	..	..
Sa	5	12	19	26	..	Sa	3	10	17	24	31	Sa	7	14	21	28	..	..

		JULY						AUGUST						SEPTEMBER			
Su	..	T^7	T^8	T^9	T^{10}	Su	..	T^{11}	T^{12}	T^{13}	T^{14}	T^{15}	Su	..	T^{16}	T^{17}	T^{18}	T^{19}	..
M	..	7	14	21	28	M	..	4	11	18	25	M	1	8	15	22	29	..
Tu	1	8	15	22	29	Tu	..	5	12	19	26	Tu	2	9	16	23	30	..
W	2	9	16	23	30	W	..	6	13	20	27	W	3	10	17	24	..	..
Th	3	10	17	24	31	Th	..	7	14	21	28	Th	4	11	18	25	..	..
F	4	11	18	25	..	F	1	8	15	22	29	F	5	12	19	26	..	..
Sa	5	12	19	26	..	Sa	2	9	16	23	30	Sa	6	13	20	27	..	..

		OCTOBER						NOVEMBER						DECEMBER			
Su	..	T^{20}	T^{21}	T^{22}	T^L	Su	..	A^{-4}	A^{-3}	A^{-2}	A^{-1}	A^1	Su	..	A^2	A^3	A^4	X^1	..
M	..	6	13	20	27	M	..	3	10	17	24	M	1	8	15	22	29	..
Tu	..	7	14	21	28	Tu	..	4	11	18	25	Tu	2	9	16	23	30	..
W	1	8	15	22	29	W	..	5	12	19	26	W	3	10	17	24	31	..
Th	2	9	16	23	30	Th	..	6	13	20	27	Th	4	11	18	X	..	..
F	3	10	17	24	31	F	..	7	14	21	28	F	5	12	19	26	..	..
Sa	4	11	18	25	..	Sa	AS	8	15	22	29	Sa	6	13	20	27	..	..

A = Ash Wednesday, Ascension, Advent
A^- = Before Advent
A^{-1} = Christ the King
A^{-4} = also All Saints (if trans.)
An = Annunciation
AS = All Saints
B = Baptism
E = Epiphany, Easter
G = Good Friday
L = Lent
L^- = Before Lent
L^{-1} = also Presentation (if trans.)
M = Maundy Thursday
P = Palm Sunday
Pr = Presentation
T = Trinity
(T^6 = also Peter and Paul, 2008)
(T^{14} = also Bartholomew, 2008)
(T^{17} = also Holy Cross Day, 2008)
(T^{18} = also Matthew, 2008)
T^L = Last Sunday after Trinity
W = Pentecost (Whit Sunday)
X = Christmas
(X^1 = also Holy Innocents, 2008)

CALENDAR 2009

		JANUARY							FEBRUARY							MARCH				
Su	..	X²	B	E²	E³	..	Su	E⁴	L⁻³	L⁻²	L⁻¹	..	..	Su	L¹	L²	L³	L⁴	L⁵	..
M	..	5	12	19	26	..	M	Pr	9	16	23	..	..	M	2	9	16	23	30	..
Tu	..	6	13	20	27	..	Tu	3	10	17	24	..	..	Tu	3	10	17	24	31	..
W	..	7	14	21	28	..	W	4	11	18	A	..	..	W	4	11	18	An	..	..
Th	1	8	15	22	29	..	Th	5	12	19	26	..	..	Th	5	12	19	26	..	..
F	2	9	16	23	30	..	F	6	13	20	27	..	..	F	6	13	20	27	..	..
Sa	3	10	17	24	31	..	Sa	7	14	21	28	..	..	Sa	7	14	21	28	..	..

		APRIL							MAY							JUNE				
Su	..	P	E	E²	E³	..	Su	..	E⁴	E⁵	E⁶	E⁷	W	Su	..	T	T¹	T²	T³	..
M	..	6	13	20	27	..	M	..	4	11	18	25	..	M	1	8	15	22	29	..
Tu	..	7	14	21	28	..	Tu	..	5	12	19	26	..	Tu	2	9	16	23	30	..
W	1	8	15	22	29	..	W	..	6	13	20	27	..	W	3	10	17	24	..	..
Th	2	M	16	23	30	..	Th	..	7	14	A	28	..	Th	4	11	18	25	..	..
F	3	G	17	24	..	..	F	1	8	15	22	29	..	F	5	12	19	26	..	..
Sa	4	11	18	25	..	..	Sa	2	9	16	23	30	..	Sa	6	13	20	27	..	..

		JULY							AUGUST							SEPTEMBER				
Su	..	T⁴	T⁵	T⁶	T⁷	..	Su	..	T⁸	T⁹	T¹⁰	T¹¹	T¹²	Su	..	T¹³	T¹⁴	T¹⁵	T¹⁶	..
M	..	6	13	20	27	..	M	..	3	10	17	24	31	M	..	7	14	21	28	..
Tu	..	7	14	21	28	..	Tu	..	4	11	18	25	..	Tu	1	8	15	22	29	..
W	1	8	15	22	29	..	W	..	5	12	19	26	..	W	2	9	16	23	30	..
Th	2	9	16	23	30	..	Th	..	6	13	20	27	..	Th	3	10	17	24	..	..
F	3	10	17	24	31	..	F	..	7	14	21	28	..	F	4	11	18	25	..	..
Sa	4	11	18	25	..	..	Sa	1	8	15	22	29	..	Sa	5	12	19	26	..	..

		OCTOBER							NOVEMBER							DECEMBER				
Su	..	T¹⁷	T¹⁸	T¹⁹	Tᴸ	..	Su	AS	A⁻³	A⁻²	A⁻¹	A¹	..	Su	..	A²	A³	A⁴	X¹	..
M	..	5	12	19	26	..	M	2	9	16	23	30	..	M	..	7	14	21	28	..
Tu	..	6	13	20	27	..	Tu	3	10	17	24	..	..	Tu	1	8	15	22	29	..
W	..	7	14	21	28	..	W	4	11	18	25	..	..	W	2	9	16	23	30	..
Th	1	8	15	22	29	..	Th	5	12	19	26	..	..	Th	3	10	17	24	31	..
F	2	9	16	23	30	..	F	6	13	20	27	..	..	F	4	11	18	X	..	..
Sa	3	10	17	24	31	..	Sa	7	14	21	28	..	..	Sa	5	12	19	26	..	..

A = Ash Wednesday, Ascension, Advent
A⁻ = Before Advent
A⁻¹ = Christ the King
An = Annunciation
AS = All Saints
B = Baptism
E = Epiphany, Easter
(E³ = also Conversion of Paul, 2009)
E⁴ = also Presentation (if trans.)
G = Good Friday
L = Lent
L⁻ = Before Lent
M = Maundy Thursday
P = Palm Sunday
Pr = Presentation
T = Trinity
(T¹⁹ = also Luke, 2009)
W = Pentecost (Whit Sunday)
X = Christmas (X¹ = also John, 2009)